ISRAEL RESTORED

By

DAVID HAMSHIRE

WIPF & STOCK · Eugene, Oregon

Wipf and Stock Publishers
199 W 8th Ave, Suite 3
Eugene, OR 97401

Israel Restored
By Hamshire, David
Copyright©2017 Apostolos
ISBN 13: 978-1-5326-6926-2
Publication date 9/23/2018
Previously published by Apostolos, 2017

TO THE JEWISH PEOPLE GOD SAID

*"Then you shall dwell in the land
that I gave to your fathers;
you shall be My people,
and I will be your God."*

(Ezekiel 36:28)

ACKNOWLEDGMENTS

As with my other book which is being published by Apostolos Publishing – *'Hebrew Foundations of the Christian Faith'* – I thank Yahweh (God's Hebrew name) for helping me in my research of the historical background to the restoration of the State of Israel. I am aware that Israel does not enjoy universal acceptance, but I do believe that Israel – despite not honoring God in the way that it should – still has an important role to play in the days in which we live.

I thank Richard Sexton for his advice regarding the final text for this book and for writing the Foreword. Richard's suggestions have added much to the original manuscript and his comments in the Foreword are more than I could have expected.

There are many who have contributed to this book, not least those who I have quoted, and there is a full bibliography at the end of this book; plus there are others who I would like to thank.

I thank Janet, my wife, for her tireless support during the fifty-plus years we have been married. Janet and I have always retained an active interest in Israel and its physical and spiritual journey, and we have shared our interest in meetings, discussions, personal Bible study and during a number of visits to Israel.

There are, of course, other contributors who I cannot name, for their names have been lost in the mist of time. After years of attendance at meetings – especially in a chapel in Bradenstoke, near Swindon, where Colin and his wife Sylvia Sinclair are joint pastors of Bradenstoke Baptist Church – I now look upon these times and these people as being crucial; for they have added real value to my knowledge and understanding of Israel.

Sometimes, a brief comment has resonated with my conviction that we have been called to do God's will. This has happened many times and without stating the obvious (what they actually said!) I wish to thank Tim Woodward who was the first to encourage me to put my hand to writing; Brian Thring, our daughter Elizabeth's father-in-law, for an off-the-cuff remark; and Roger Hitchings, who opened my thoughts to a scripture I had not previously considered.

Lastly, I thank Mathew Bartlett – Commissioning Editor of Apostolos Publishing – for his trust in my ability to add to his excellent portfolio of titles. Publishing new titles is no easy task, and so I wish to thank Mathew for his encouragement to keep going! Although at times study and the recording of facts and figures can be arduous, writing is something I enjoy – and more so if it helps the reader to understand Israel.

David Hamshire

AUTHOR'S NOTES

Within the text of this book where I have quoted Scripture I have done so using italics. In some places I have used bold type; whilst at other times I have underlined a scripture to show how it has helped me in my thought process. The reason I have done this is to assist the reader in understanding the scriptures I refer to – and importantly, their context.

I have two additional comments. First, this book is positive about the Jews and Israel – subjects I know to be controversial. If the reader should disagree with a part of its content, or the thrust of its argument, then I would ask the reader to respect the fact that the Bible has been my main source for this book's focus.

My other comment concerns the word: *'Exegesis'*. My dictionary tells me it is the word used for giving explanation – especially from the Bible. When others use this word I tend to shudder! The reason, possibly, is because my life has followed a very basic path in the way I seek to understand the Bible; I do so from a lay-person's perspective. Whatever your status (and I'm all for scholarly achievement), for the sake of the Jews and Israel, I commend this book to you.

David Hamshire
January 2017

CONTENTS

ACKNOWLEDGMENTS ··································· 4

AUTHOR'S NOTES ···································· 6

PREFACE ··· 10

INTRODUCTION ···································· 14

THE LAND OF ISRAEL ······························ 22

THE PEOPLE OF ISRAEL ···························· 40

ACRIMONY – BITTERNESS ·························· 64

CAN A NATION BE BORN IN A DAY? ············ 82

A THIRD SIGN – LAZARUS ························ 100

LESSONS FROM HISTORY ·························· 120

ISRAEL'S DECLARATION OF INDEPENDENCE
·· 142

ABOUT THE AUTHOR ····························· 150

BIBLIOGRAPHY ···································· 154

HEBREW FOUNDATIONS OF THE CHRISTIAN
FAITH ·· 156

FOREWORD

The mention of *'Israel'* usually provokes a reaction of some sort. In today's world, the reaction is often negative, with many regarding the nation of Israel as an obstacle to peace, and peace in the Middle East in particular. I believe that such reactions are promoted by biased reports coming out of an anti-Semitic news station in the Middle East, and such propaganda being uncritically supported and broadcast by national media throughout the Western world.

Among the Christian community, there is sometimes a similar polarising in people's opinions of Jews as a people and Israel as a nation. On the one hand there are a few who are deeply envious of the Jews and their traditions and would give anything to be able to become Jewish! At the other extreme are those who espouse *'Replacement Theology'* and regard Israel as a distraction compared with the true church and God's purposes for it. Israel, it seems, provokes deeply held passions in people's hearts!

This book has been written by someone who is also a man of strong passions – especially when it comes to the Jews and their nation. David Hamshire has a passion which drives him to discover a true and an eternal viewpoint with which to regard Israel. In looking for arguments to establish his belief in the central place that Israel plays in the purposes of God,

David examines Scripture with the eye of a detective, and having found gold nuggets of truth, he then seeks to substantiate them by looking at the history of Israel the nation and the Jews as a people. David also notes how history has endorsed the validity of prophetic words found in Scripture, and the teachings of Jesus and the writings of the Apostles.

The result is a thesis which presents watertight arguments, insightful interpretations, and consistent evidence of a nation which still occupies a place in God's purposes. Its non-existence from the AD 70's, its subsequent resurrection in the twentieth century, and its survival in recent wars in which it has been vastly outnumbered by invading forces, all speak of a nation which still has God's hand upon it.

'ISRAEL RESTORED' is an argument for the place of Israel in the heart of God, which is detailed and persuasive. David presents a coordinated stream of scriptural support for the survival of Israel against all odds, and the place of Israel in these end-times. After reading this book, it would be difficult to hold an anti-Semitic view of Israel, or to still consider that the emergence of the Church has done away with Israel as far as God is concerned.

I commend this book to you.

Richard G. Sexton
Bath, England

PREFACE

My aim in publishing this book has been to provide a biblical perspective of Israel the people and their land. The Bible, therefore, has been my main literary source for the contents included in this book.

Whilst some of the material I have used originated from others, my objective has been to review certain prophetic (biblical) statements; then to link these statements to historical events concerning Israel. Israel is a small country, a disputed country, and some in the Middle East (and elsewhere) would not be sorry to witness Israel's demise. But why should a nation such as Israel, so small compared to other countries, and with such a mixed ethnic population, be the focus of such antipathy and persecution?

Israel today has its supporters and its opponents, and for those who are not sure who is right, what I have attempted to do is to explain Israel from what (I believe) is God's viewpoint. Because the Bible should be for those who believe in God their reference, I list on the following pages, three promises which are fundamental regarding the nation of Israel.

God's Promise to Abraham

The Lord said to His friend Abraham, after Lot had separated himself from Abraham: *"Lift your eyes now* *and look from the place where you are – northward, southward, eastward, and westward; for all the land which you see I give to you and your descendants <u>forever</u>. And I will make your descendants as the dust on the earth; so that if a man could number the dust of the earth, then your descendants also could be numbered. Arise, walk in the land through its length and its width, for I give it to you"* (Genesis 13:14–17).

God's Promise to Jacob

'*And behold, the LORD stood above it* [a ladder which stretched from earth to heaven] *and said: "I am the LORD God of Abraham your father and the God of Isaac; the land on which you lie I will give it to you and your descendants. Also your descendants shall be as the dust of the earth; you shall spread abroad to the west and east, to the north and south; and in you and in your seed all the families of the earth shall be blessed"'* (Genesis 28:13–14).

God's Promise to Israel

"For you are a holy people to the LORD your God; the LORD your God has chosen you to be a people for Himself, a special treasure above all the peoples on the face of the earth. The LORD did not set His love on you nor choose you because you were more in number than any other people, for you were the least of all peoples; but because the LORD loves you, and because He would keep the oath which He swore to your fathers, the LORD has brought you out with a

mighty hand, and redeemed you from the house of bondage, from Pharaoh king of Egypt."

"Therefore, know that the LORD your God, He is God, the faithful God who keeps covenant and mercy for a thousand generations with those who love Him and keep his commandments" (Deuteronomy 7:6–9).

****

PSALM 46 – ISRAEL'S DEPENDANCY ON GOD

'God is our refuge and strength, a very present help in trouble. Therefore we will not fear even though the earth be removed, and though the mountains be carried into the midst of the sea; though its waters roar and be troubled, though the mountains shake with its swelling.' [Selah].

'There is a river whose streams shall make glad the city of God, the holy place of the tabernacle of the Most High. God is in the midst of her, she shall not be moved; God shall help her, just at the break of dawn. The nations raged, the kingdoms were moved; He uttered His voice, the earth melted.'

'The LORD of hosts is with us; the God of Jacob is our refuge.' [Selah].

'Come, behold the works of the LORD, who has made desolations in the earth. He makes wars to cease to the end of the earth; He breaks the bow and cuts the spear in two; He burns the chariot in the fire. Be still and know that I am God; I will be exalted among the nations, I will be exalted in the earth! The LORD of hosts is with us; the God of Jacob is our refuge.' [Selah].

INTRODUCTION

From the list of some of my earliest memories there are two images I have not been able to erase. As a youth, I can still remember obtaining at a church jumble sale, an illustrated volume of the Second World War. The book was a photographic record of a war which had baffled many, and which had led to an estimated fifty five million people being killed.

It had been a war which had caused much suffering throughout the world. Not only had people died, but the war had caused many to be left as widows and orphans. Among those who had been injured, many would be maimed for the rest of their lives. In terms of loss of life and personal injury, and also material damage, the war had been a very costly war and its impact had been far reaching.

After the war, for those who had been traumatized by what they had experienced, photographs would have lacked any realism as to the horror of war – their memories would have been much more vivid.

Of the many illustrations of war, my book contained two photographs that illustrated the brutality of what has been described as the Holocaust – the destruction of Europe's Jews. The two photographs were of two trenches, and in each trench were placed the naked

Introduction

and interlocking corpses of thousands of Jews – men, women and children. Although I was only a youth, nevertheless, I still wanted to know why this mass murder of Jewish people had taken place.

From the time when I first saw those two images, I have tried to fathom the reason why Jewish people had been killed and their bodies consigned to mass graves. War is usually lethal, but this was not war; this was genocide. Possibly, because of my naivety, I was confused; I didn't understand. I knew nations might go to war for reasons of territorial or political dispute, but why kill people because they are of a different ethnicity? Why had such suffering been inflicted on Jewish people, a crime which can only be described as the mass murder of the innocents? It seemed there was no logical explanation for what had happened to these vulnerable people, nearly all of them civilians. And my parents were reluctant to help me understand. In the years after the war, its politics and its consequences were rarely discussed.

It has taken me decades to comprehend the evil of anti-Semitism (and I'm not sure if I fully understand the reasons for it now), but from the time when I first saw those two images of a few of the victims of the Holocaust, I have held a profound respect for Jewish people. The reason, possibly, is because as I have discovered, for nearly 2,000 years, Jewish people have been regularly and cruelly persecuted by non-Jewish people. In other words, the Gentile world has treated them badly. Was it a case that Europe's Jews had been selected for racial extermination – Hitler's final solution – because their religion was different to that of their oppressors, or was there another agenda? At the time and for whatever reason, it was one that I was ignorant of.

Among most Gentile communities – even Christian communities – those who support the Jewish people are usually in a minority. But why are so many so antagonistic towards Jewish people when they have contributed so much to agriculture, economics, literature, medicine and physics? And, it has to be said, that internationally, during the last one hundred years, their achievements have earned them more than one hundred and twenty Nobel prizes.

There are today about fourteen million Jewish people in the world – about 0.02% of the world's population. In a wide range of subjects the Jewish contribution to humanity is significantly out of proportion to their numbers; an achievement not equaled by any other nation or people group.

The Bible's Theme

It was in 1980 I began to record nine joined-up words that I saw as being the Bible's central theme. The references I took note of are like a red line running through the pages of Scripture. These profound words describe the result of having a genuine relationship

Introduction

with God. In other words they are foundational to our understanding of the Bible's message. Of the many who contributed to the Bible, the majority of them wrote about this fundamental truth. Therefore, in references such as Exodus 6:7; Jeremiah 30:22; Ezekiel 36:28 and 37:23; Hosea 1:9 and 2:23; Zechariah 8:8; 2 Corinthians 6:16; Hebrews 8:10 and Revelation 21:3; we read these words: *"I am your God and you are My people."*

There are many other passages in the Bible which restate this fundamental truth; and because of this, this concise statement has led me to conclude that from the very beginning of man's existence, God has been seeking to nurture a close relationship with all who are willing to respect Him, trust Him and obey Him – be they Jew or Gentile. It is how God related to Adam and Eve in the Garden of Eden before they sinned

It was also true when the time came for Moses to lead Jacob's descendants out of Egypt. For four hundred years the children of Israel had endured slavery at the hands of the Egyptians. However, God heard their prayers and sent to them His servant Moses, that they might return to the land He had promised them. At the time when the children of Israel left Egypt, a mixed multitude of other people (Exodus 12:38) also left, for they wanted to accompany God's people and journey with them to the promised land; a land which one day would become known to them and their descendants as Israel. After their departure from Egypt, God said to them: *"You have seen what I did to the Egyptians, and how I bore you on eagles' wings and brought you to Myself. Now therefore, if you will indeed obey My voice and keep My covenant, then you shall be a special treasure to Me above all people; for all the earth is Mine. And you shall be a kingdom of priests and a holy nation"* (Exodus 19:4–6).

Has God Abandoned the Jews?

During the time of Moses, because of disobedience, God came close to abandoning His people (Exodus 32:9–10). So has God now abandoned the Jews in favour of the Gentiles? If God has abandoned them, can God be trusted to keep His covenant with Gentile believers who today claim to be His people?

Just how trustworthy is the God who Christians claim to serve if He has reneged on His covenant with Abraham; when God said to him: *"Get out of your country, from your family and from your father's house, to a land that I will show you. I will make of you a great nation; I will bless you and make your name great; and you shall be a blessing. I will bless those who bless you, I will curse him who curses you; and in you all the families of the earth shall be blessed."* (Genesis 12:1–3).

Israel Today

Since 1948, when Israel again became a nation state, approved of by the United Nations (29th November

Introduction

1947), hundreds have written about the land of Israel and its people; so is there more needing to be said?

Within the following pages, readers may recognize some of the facts I refer to, but there may be some material that is new, especially where Jesus speaks to four of His disciples about Israel's dispersion (see Mark chapter 13 where Jesus describes the destruction of Israel's temple which took place in 70 CE when the Romans destroyed Jerusalem). However, it was not only in His words, but in some of the practical things which Jesus did that confirmed His understanding of Israel's impending destruction; a destruction which was to be followed by a second period of exile and a second restoration (as prophesied by Ezekiel).

Israel, a democratic country, is not about to evaporate. If God who has for the second time re-gathered His ancient people to their land, was to again oversee their destruction, my faith in God would be severely tested.

Whilst I have noted in the Bible many references to Israel's restoration in the so-called *'Last Days'*, I have not been able to locate any suggestion of a third dispersion of the Jewish people, or of their total and final destruction. The fact so many Jewish people are once again living in the promised land, confirms what God said would one-day happen; for it has always been God's intention that the Jewish people and the land He gave to them to inhabit, should become one, as in a marriage.

For this to have happened, although there is no easy explanation for the trauma involved in the First World War (during which ten million people died), one direct result of the war was to prepare the land for the Jews to return there. The Second World War (during which out of a total of fifty-five million deaths, six million Jewish people died), prepared the survivors (and others) to return to their former home-land.

Many have seen in these two wars, evidence that the two included God's earlier promises for His people. During these two very destructive wars – each a struggle for supremacy based on greed – which took place over a period of less than thirty-one years and which resulted in widespread chaos and destruction, God was working in a way known only to Him. For those who may not (or who cannot) accept the outcome from the twentieth century's two major world-wide conflicts as being a part of God's plan for Israel, then there is a need to look much deeper into God's Word. It is here the prophetic scenario which has been played out over the last one hundred years can be seen, and is why I have applied my mind and my study to these things.

The Bible, completed nearly two thousand years ago, has stood the test of time and has exposed man's basic failure – his reluctance to relate to the God who made him. Not only can the Bible on examination be shown to be reliable, the Bible can also prove that what God has said will one day happen to His people and to His land, either has happened, or it will eventually come to pass.

As a result of my study of the Bible and observation of history (its triumphs and its tragedies, its ups and its downs) in the following chapters I have sought to explain something of what I have learnt and relate these conclusions to a Biblical perspective of Israel and the Jewish people. This is why I have referred to this book's title as: *'ISRAEL RESTORED'*.

****

THE LAND OF ISRAEL

There are, I have been told, over seven hundred verses in the Old Testament (known by Jewish people as the *'Tanakh'*) which establishes a direct and a permanent link between the land of Israel and the Jewish people. The following three verses from the book of the prophet Jeremiah are unequivocal.

'Thus says the LORD, who gives the sun for a light by day, the ordinances of the moon and the stars for a light by night, who disturbs the sea, and its waves roar (the LORD of hosts is His name): "If those ordinances depart from before Me, says the LORD, then the seed of Israel shall also cease from being a nation before Me forever." Thus says the LORD: "If heaven above can be measured, and the foundations of the earth searched out beneath, I will also cast off all the seed of Israel for all that they have done, says the LORD" ' (Jeremiah 31:35–37).

The sun, moon and stars remain fixed in the positions in which they were once placed (one of the reasons is for them to act as *'signs'* – Genesis 1:14), and man continues in his relentless search to discover how vast the universe is and what secrets the depths of the earth and the seas have yet to reveal. Jeremiah was told by God that man would never be able to discover the full extent of these secrets, and it would be on this basis

The Land of Israel

the descendants of Abraham, through his son Isaac and grandson Jacob (Israel), that they would forever be linked to the land God had prepared for them. This promise is one made by God with Abraham and with the soil of this land (Genesis 12:7). Today we know of this land as: *'Eretz Israel'*.

A scripture which has frequently been misquoted is 2 Chronicles 7:14. It reads as follows: *"If My people who are called by My name will humble themselves* [that they respect God], *and pray and seek My face* [that they trust God], *and turn from their wicked ways* [that they obey God], *then I will hear from heaven, and will forgive their sin and heal their land."*

Here God says He will do two things providing His people keep to the three basic steps – respect, trust and obedience. First, if they humble themselves and pray, God will listen and will forgive their sin. Second, if they turn from their wicked ways, God will heal their land. When Solomon first received this promise it was given to Israel – not to Gentiles. The land spoken of in this passage is a clear reference to and a promise concerning: *'The Land of Israel'*.

Israel is a land the Bible describes as belonging not to man – not even to the Jewish people – but to God. More than three thousand years ago, God said to Moses, *"The land shall not be sold permanently, for the land is Mine; for you are strangers and sojourners with Me"* (Leviticus 25:23).

Because God has said that this land belongs to Him, it follows that God has the right to choose who are to be its lawful custodians. Therefore, it is important that we understand the historical significance of this land, its present day situation, and its future importance – for it is God's land.

Of all the countries in the world today, Israel is one of the smallest; yet it is also the most criticized, with the criticism usually accompanied by the question: *'Who owns the land?'* It would seem the Bible is rarely referred to in order to find an answer to this question.

The Song of Moses

Deuteronomy, chapter 32, is a song written by God (Deuteronomy 31:19) and given by God to Moses. Its purpose was for Moses to teach the children of Israel about God's faithfulness before entering the promised land. The song is a record of how God had led and miraculously provided for the children of Israel during their forty years in the wilderness. But the song is also a warning of what might happen should the children of Israel no longer respect and trust God, which would lead to them disobeying God.

"Give ear, O heavens and I will speak; and hear, O earth, the words of my mouth. Let my teaching drop as the rain, my speech distil as the dew, as raindrops on the tender herb, and as showers on the grass. For I proclaim the name of the LORD."

The Land of Israel

"Ascribe greatness to our God. He is the Rock, His work is perfect, for all His ways are justice, a God of truth and without injustice; righteous and upright is He." [Verses 1–4]. *Remember the days of old, consider the years of many generations. Ask your father and he will show you; your elders and they will tell you: When the Most High divided their inheritance to the nations, when He separated the sons of Adam, He set the boundaries of the peoples according to the number of the children of Israel. For the LORD's portion is His people, Jacob is the place of His inheritance. He found him in a desert land and in the wasteland, a howling wilderness; He encircled him, He instructed him, He kept him as the apple of His eye."* [Verses 7–10].

However, if the children of Israel were to become unfaithful, God warned them saying: *"They shall be wasted with hunger, devoured by pestilence and bitter destruction; I will also send against them the teeth of beasts, with the poison of serpents of the dust. The sword shall destroy outside; there shall be terror within for the young man and virgin, the nursing child and the man of gray hairs"* [Verses 23–25]. *"For they are a nation void of counsel, nor is there any understanding in them. Oh, that they were wise, that they understood this, that they would consider their latter end!"* (Verses 28–29).

These are just a few of the lines from the Song of Moses. Moses reminded Israel that God had chosen them and had enabled them to ride in the heights of the earth that they might eat the produce of the fields and draw honey from the rock (Verse 13). However, if they forsook God and were scornful of the *'Rock of their Salvation'* (Verse 15), God would hide His face from them (Verse 20). Also, disasters would come upon them (Verse 23), *"For the LORD will judge His people"* (Verse 36). Finally, despite the inevitability of (righteous) judgment, God encourages the Gentiles to rejoice with the Hebrew people. The reason?

"He will provide atonement for His land and His people" (verse 43).

These two promises, to provide atonement for the land and atonement for its people, are indivisible. The land and the people (the Jewish people) were always intended to be a united entity – a marriage designed and approved of by God. In this context, God informed Moses that although there would be times when the land would become separated from its (Jewish) inhabitants, but not divorced, yet God would eventually provide atonement for His land and His people.

'Kaphar', the Hebrew word for atonement, occurs only in the Old Testament, but its true meaning is missing. Although the word *'Kaphar'* is not found in the New Testament, the work of atonement is and its meaning is explained: *"...the blood of Jesus Christ, God's Son, cleanses us from all sin"* (1 John 1:7).

Atonement means: *'To cleanse, or to cover'*. Moses wrote that atonement for the land and its people – to make the two clean – would one day take place.

Charles Hodge, a theologian from the 19th century, commented: *'God sometimes enters into covenant with communities. Thus he covenanted with the whole human race that the world shall not again be destroyed by a deluge, and that the seasons shall continue to succeed each other. He covenanted with the Jews to be a God to them and to their seed forever, and that they should be to Him a people.'*

One of God's most far-reaching covenants is the one He made with Abraham (Genesis 13:14–17). It is the same covenant He later reminded Moses of, and then Ezekiel. Each of God's covenants should be taken seriously, but the detail of what God revealed to Ezekiel has implications today, not only for Israel (as we shall see later), but also for the entire world.

Obedience and Disobedience – Blessings and Curses

From Scripture, it is clear that God's blessings and His judgments may have more than one fulfilment (such as those mentioned in Deuteronomy chapter 28 which lists the blessings and curses which will ensue from the Jewish people's obedience, or disobedience, with reference to God's commandments). A number of the prophesies listed in the book of Ezekiel have similar features, with some relating to the time when

Nebuchadnezzar attacked Jerusalem in 597 BCE, when the majority of those living in the city at the time were taken into exile.

Detail of a further warning which appears in Ezekiel is linked to a later event, and almost certainly applies to the second exile of the Jewish people which took place after the destruction of Jerusalem in 70 CE. The second exile of the Jewish people involved a much wider dispersion than the first, and lasted for much longer – nearly 1,900 years. Both exiles took place, and the two commenced on the same day of the same month in the Hebrew calendar – the 9th day of the month Av. This day is still regarded by Jewish people as a most solemn day and is known as: *'Tisha B'Av'*.

The period of time between the two dates from when the two exiles of the Jews commenced – the first in 597 BCE (which is 596 years, seven months and 21 days), the second in 70 CE (which is 69 years, four months and 9 days) – was <u>*exactly*</u> 666 years.

In Hebrew understanding, treble six is the number of human perfection. The author, E.W. Bullinger, writes: *'666 is the trinity of human perfection; the perfection of imperfection; the culmination of human pride in independence of God and opposition to His Christ.'*

Is this why the Jewish people became separated from their inheritance; a land which had been given to them as a sign of God's love?

The Bible teaches it was because of unfaithfulness God's people became estranged from Him; ending in separation from their land. This separation has taken place not just once, but twice, and was a consequence of serious disobedience. But also in Ezekiel 15:7, we read that Jerusalem would be destroyed by fire on two separate occasions. The first time Jerusalem was destroyed by fire was in 587 BCE. The second time was in 70 CE; thus confirming what Ezekiel wrote.

Marriage and Divorce

God's plan for marriage is that it is a union between two dissimilar parties (such as a man and a woman), and marriage means commitment and companionship, something which Israel as a nation has rarely kept. Divorce cancels both, yet marriage was not designed for divorce; and so God promised Moses He would initiate atonement in order to recover (restore) and cleanse His land and His people.

The prophet Isaiah also wrote about this when he recorded: *"It shall come to pass in that day that the Lord shall set His hand again the second time to recover the remnant of His people who are left, from Assyria and Egypt, from Pathros and Cush, from Elam and Shina, from Hamath and the islands of the sea. He will set up a banner for the nations, and will assemble the outcasts of Israel, and gather together the dispersed of Judah from the four corners of the earth"* (Isaiah 11:11–12).

Israel Restored

Israel as a nation has been involved in two separations and two restorations (the last commenced officially in 1948), and each has involved both the land and the Jewish people.

Later in Isaiah's writings, we read that God said He would establish a restored relationship (marriage) between His land and its people: *"For Zion's sake I will not hold My peace. And for Jerusalem's sake I will not rest, until her righteousness goes forth as brightness, and her salvation as a lamp that burns. The Gentiles shall see your righteousness, and all kings your glory. You shall be called by a new name* [as when a lady marries a man she changes her name to that of her husband], *which the mouth of the Lord will name. You shall also be a crown of glory in the hand of the Lord, and a royal diadem in the hand of your God. You shall no longer be termed Forsaken, nor shall your land any more be called Desolate; but you shall be called Hephzibah, and your land Beulah;* [literally, *'My delight is in her'* or *'Married'*] *For the Lord delights in you, and your land shall be married. For as a young man marries a virgin, so shall your sons marry you; and as the bridegroom rejoices over the bride, so shall your God rejoice over you"* (Isaiah 62:1-5).

God informed Isaiah He reserved the right to have the final say about how the land of Israel and its people would be brought together again. Regarding marriage, Jesus said: *"What God has joined together, let not*

The Land of Israel

man separate" (Matthew 19:6). I realise His response was directed to the Pharisees who questioned Him about marital divorce; but divorce can also apply to God's commitment and His companionship with the land of Israel and the Jewish people.

Since Israel's Declaration of Independence in 1948, many (including the United Nations) have tried to influence Israel's government into making territorial concessions for the sake of peace. The problem is that when you have so little land to give away, it's hard to give away what you do have. It is also made harder when those who are doing the demanding are not your friends but your sworn enemies; those who have consistently refused to recognize Israel's right to exist. For Israel to concede land for peace would be to countenance a separation of the people from the land – a type of divorce. It would also weaken Israel's ability to protect its people.

In the title of this book I refer to Israel as having the status of a restored nation. The validity for this is supported by the biblical narrative which shows how God has twice found it necessary to exile Israel as a punishment for its wrongdoing; then to Israel's benefit – the restoration of the Jewish people to their land and a renewed relationship with their God.

God has always had a restored Israel as His objective and continues to work tirelessly and graciously towards this; that Israel (as well as Gentile believers in Jesus) might become His people. For this to happen, God (because God is holy), has to discipline us when we do wrong, as a good father disciplines his children. God's purpose is to bless in order that we may be partakers of His holiness (Hebrews 12:5–11). Although it is sadly inevitable that most people do not want to share God's holiness; nevertheless, for those who wish to know the creator of the universe and His Son the Lord Jesus, and to know the power of the Holy Spirit in their lives, God's discipline is the means whereby we become trained to live holy lives.

Israel's prophets were instructed to warn Israel of the consequences of not allowing God to guide them. Not only would a negative response impact on their personal lives, it would also affect how the land God had given them would respond to God's blessing. As we have seen, Ezekiel was one of God's prophets, and his writings include both positive and negative statements, indicating how God would deal with His people and His land – His blessing and His curses.

Ezekiel 36:1–12

"And you, son of man, prophesy to the mountains of Israel, and say, 'O mountains of Israel, hear the word of the LORD! Thus says the LORD GOD: "Because the enemy has said of you, 'Aha! The ancient heights have become our possession,' "therefore prophesy, and say: 'Thus says the LORD GOD: "<u>Because they made you desolate</u> and swallowed you up on every

side, so that you became the possession of the rest of the nations, and you are taken up by the lips of talkers and slandered by the people" – 'therefore, O mountains of Israel, hear the word of the LORD GOD! Thus says the LORD GOD to the mountains, the hills, the rivers, the valleys, the desolate wastes, and the cities that have been forsaken, which became plunder and mockery to the rest of the nations all around – therefore thus says the LORD GOD: "Surely I have spoken in My burning jealousy against the rest of the nations and against all Edom, who gave my land to themselves as a possession with wholehearted joy and spiteful minds, in order to plunder its open country. Therefore prophesy concerning the land of Israel, and say to the mountains, the hills, the rivers, and the valleys, 'Thus says the Lord GOD: "Behold, I have spoken in My jealousy and My fury, because you have borne the shame of the nations." Therefore thus says the LORD GOD: "I have raised My hand in an oath that surely the nations that are around you shall bear their own shame. But you, O mountains of Israel, you shall shoot forth your branches and yield your fruit to My people Israel, for they are about to come. For indeed I am for you, and I will turn to you, and you shall be tilled and sown. I will multiply men upon you, all the house of Israel, all of it; and the cities shall be inhabited and the ruins rebuilt. I will multiply upon you man and beast; and they shall increase and bear young; I will make you inhabited as in former times, and do better for you than at your beginnings. Then you will know that I am the LORD. Yes, I will cause men to walk on you, My people Israel; they shall take possession of you, and you shall be their inheritance; no more shall you bereave them of children."

God is speaking here to Ezekiel, who then restates God's covenant with the land of Israel. Ezekiel is told to prophesy to the mountains, hills, rivers and valleys, the desolate places and the cities which other nations would one day plunder. God said a day was coming when the nations of the world would cause the land of Israel to become barren, forsaken and despised.

Mark Twain

In 1867 the American writer Mark Twain embarked on a pilgrimage to the land promised to Abraham. Then it was known as Palestine, but it was also known as the Holy Land. Recalling his experience, Twain wrote: *"Palestine sits in sackcloth and ashes, desolate and unlovely. Nazareth is forlorn. Jericho the accursed lies a moldering ruin. Bethlehem and Bethany, in their poverty and their humiliation, have nothing about them now to remind one that they once knew the high honour of the Saviour's presence."*

Describing the Jezreel Valley, the site of ancient battles, Twain went on to say: *"There is not a solitary village throughout its whole extent, not for thirty miles in either direction. There are two or three small clusters of Bedouin tents, but not a single permanent habitation."*

In the late nineteenth and early twentieth centuries, when Jewish people in significant numbers began to make their way to Palestine, much of the northern area around the Sea of Galilee was a vast swamp, riddled with disease and was totally unsuitable for any human habitation. Many of the early settlers died as a result of hazards, including malaria, which were endemic in the region. Why did these early settlers risk their lives, and also the lives of their families, in seeking to reclaim this neglected and barren land? Was it because God had said that His people would one day return to their original homeland, and that it would again become tilled and habitable?

Until comparatively recently, the land of Israel was a land which was unloved. Centuries of domination by foreign powers had left it in a state of ruin – precisely as Ezekiel had prophesied. When Turkey ruled this land (until 1917), it imposed a tax on the trees. In order to reduce their taxes, most of those who lived in the land cut down the majority of the trees! Such senseless destruction only compounded the land's neglect and infertility.

A Curious Illustration

Included in the detail of God's covenant with the land of Israel as made known to Ezekiel, there exists a curious illustration. If you, too, regard this illustration as a little unusual, then it is important to remember it was God who provided the illustration, not Ezekiel. The illustration God chose is described in the same chapter of Ezekiel as previously quoted. It is as follows: *"Son of man, when the house of Israel dwelt in their own land, they defiled it by their own ways and deeds; to Me their way was like the uncleanness of a woman in her customary impurity"* (Ezekiel 36:17).

Why did God chose this illustration? Surely, Jewish women must have felt some degree of shame when they were treated as being impure, or unclean, at the time of their period of menstruation? That God should refer to this natural occurrence for His illustration is one we shall return to later, for it has a remarkable application.

A woman's husband (if she was married), her family and the rest of her community, all knew what was being implied when labeled unclean. I know of no reason why this normal physical occurrence should have been looked upon in this way. But whatever the reason, the Bible states that with the advent of the Mosaic Law, Jewish women were considered as being unclean during their menstruation period. Also, this would have included her bed, her chair and any item she came into contact with. Her personal possessions, everything, was treated as she was treated; they were looked upon as being unclean.

The Land of Israel

"Every bed on which she lies all the days of her discharge shall be to her as the bed of her impurity; and whatever she sits on shall be unclean, as the uncleanness of her impurity. Whoever touches those things shall be unclean; he shall wash his clothes and bathe in water, and be unclean until the evening" (Leviticus 15:26–27).

What is relevant from this illustration is to note how God's description of the future state of the land of Israel will be akin to the physical condition which women in Israel knew of from personal experience. However, God said He would not abandon the land or consider it as permanently unclean. God promised His people that eventually they would be able to return to the land and that on the mountains, the trees would produce fruit. Ezekiel prophesied (or talked) to the trees!

The Restoration of Israel

In 1948 when the modern state of Israel came into existence, in just a few months over 800,000 Jews were forced to pack their bags with only a few belongings and flee from neighboring Arab lands. Most of their possessions, including a great deal of property, was confiscated by the Arab states.

From Baghdad alone, 124,638 Jews were forced to flee as a result of deliberately provoked persecution. Many of those who were forced to leave this ancient city, after centuries of assimilation, may have recalled the massacre (*Pogrom*) of Jews which had taken place in Baghdad during the night, $1^{st} - 2^{nd}$ June, 1941, when at least 180 Jews were killed and hundreds more were injured. The consequences of this gave context to the declaration of the *'Voice of Israel Radio'* at the time: *"It is impossible for Jews to live among Muslims."* In more recent times, Iran and other Arab nations have called for the liquidation of Israel.

It is almost certainly true that a number of the world's leaders would like to see Israel destroyed, or as a recent Iranian President once called for: *"That all Israelis be cast into the sea!"*

Political leaders (and others) from around the world who oppose Israel, would do well to note the position taken by Gamaliel. When Peter was brought before the Jewish Council for preaching and healing in the name of Jesus, Gamaliel's advice was that they should refrain from punishing him, for he knew that if what the apostles were doing was God's work, then the Council might become involved in opposing God – and Gamaliel knew they could never win!

There are still some today who have yet to grasp this principle; therefore, they would do well to recall that if they oppose Israel's right to exist, or try to divide the land by forcing Israel to concede territory, then to some degree they are opposing God. The reason is the land of Israel, including the Jewish people, are part of

The Land of Israel

God's plan for the world. They are a people who have been chosen by God in order that the land, and they, too, might become cleansed.

Cleansing, or atonement, is the word God used when He told Moses of what would eventually take place in this land and to its people. I know of no other place where God has an important reason for making it clean, so that when Jesus makes His final appearance, it will be a land ready and fit for the *'King of Kings'*.

This brings us to consider Ezekiel's next vision which was inspired by God. For those who are familiar with the Bible it is sometimes referred to as: *'The Valley of Dry Bones'* – and this time it concerns the people of the land of Israel, the Jewish people.

****

THE PEOPLE OF ISRAEL

If Ezekiel chapter thirty six is a statement about God's promises with and for the land of Israel, then Ezekiel chapter thirty seven is a statement about His promises with regard to the people of Israel – the Hebrew, or Jewish people.

Ezekiel 37:1–11

'The hand of the LORD came upon me and brought me out in the Spirit of the LORD, and set me down in the midst of the valley; and it was full of bones. Then He caused me to pass by them all around, and behold, there were very many in the open valley; and indeed they were very dry. And He said to me, "Son of man, can these bones live?"So I answered, "O LORD GOD, You know." Again He said to me, "Prophesy to these bones and say to them, 'O dry bones, hear the word of the LORD! Thus says the LORD GOD to these bones: "Surely I will cause breath to enter into you, and you shall live. I will put sinews on you and bring flesh upon you, cover you with skin and put breath in you; and you shall live. Then you shall know that I am the LORD." So I prophesied as I was commanded; and as I prophesied, there was a noise, and suddenly a rattling; and the bones came together, bone to bone. Indeed, as I looked, the sinews and the flesh came upon them, and the skin covered them

*over; but there was no breath in them. Also He said to me, "Prophesy to the breath, prophesy, son of man, and say to the breath, thus says the LORD GOD: Come from the four winds, O breath, and breathe on these slain, that they may live." So I prophesied as He commanded me, and breath came into them, and they lived, and stood upon their feet, an exceeding great army. Then He said to me, "**<u>Son of man, these bones are the whole house of Israel</u>**. They indeed say, our bones are dry, our hope is lost, and we ourselves are cut off!"'* (emphasis added by the author).

In verse three of this passage in Ezekiel, a question is asked: *"Son of man, can these bones live?"* It is God who asks the question. Ezekiel had no idea whether the bones could live or not live. God, however, knew the bones could live, and that one day He would fulfil His promise and cause life to enter them.

God's question about the bones and their ability to come to life and live again is of vital significance, as is God's illustration of the woman I referred to in the previous chapter; for in their fulfilment the two are closely related.

I quote from Joseph Hunting's book *'Israel, a Modern Miracle'* and his thoughts concerning Israel:

'The great nation of Israel, that once knew the secret of supernatural power under the leadership of Joshua, David and Samuel, became scattered as dry

bones among the nations after the Romans destroyed Jerusalem in 70 A.D.'

For some (as I hinted earlier) Deuteronomy 28 has become known as the Old Testament's blessings and curses chapter – but this is somewhat misleading. A more accurate description might be the obedience and disobedience chapter. The blessings and the curses are the consequences, for they relate to the issues which are at stake – namely: Obedience and Disobedience.

In the second part of Deuteronomy 28, the part that describes the curses, Moses appears to state that if Israel persistently refuses to obey God, then its people will experience two major periods of judgment. The first judgment (verses 36–48), corresponds to the first exile of the Jews to Babylon, which commenced in 597 BCE. The second judgment of the Jews (verses 49–61), anticipates a much harsher and longer lasting period of foreign exile.

In about the year 75 CE, the noted Jewish historian Josephus, published his manuscript *'The Jewish War'*, in which he describes the siege and fall of Jerusalem. Josephus recorded that during the siege – which took place from 66 to 70 CE – a million Jewish people died. When the Romans first laid siege to Jerusalem, the siege commenced at the time of the Hebrew festival of Passover, and was why so many Jewish people were in Jerusalem. Around fifteen hundred years before the siege commenced, it was recorded in

Deuteronomy that Moses had informed the children of Israel: *"You shall be left few in number, whereas you were as the stars of heaven in multitude, because you would not obey the voice of the LORD your God"* (Deuteronomy 28:62) In verses 63–67, Moses goes on to describe how only a few will survive the siege, and that they will then be scattered to the ends of the earth.

"And you shall be plucked from off the land which you go to possess. Then the LORD will scatter you among all peoples, from one end of the earth to the other, and there you shall serve other gods, which neither you nor your fathers have known – wood and stone. And among those nations you shall find no rest, nor shall the sole of your foot have a resting place; but there the LORD will give you a trembling heart, failing eyes, and anguish of soul. Your life shall hang in doubt before you; you shall fear day and night, and have no assurance of life. In the morning you shall say, 'Oh that it were evening!' And at evening you shall say, 'Oh, that it were morning!' because of the fear which terrifies your heart, and because of the sight which your eyes see." What Moses described did eventually happen.

Leo Pinsker

In 1882, the Polish-born Jew, Leo Pinsker, argued that Jews could not be assimilated in other nations because they belonged elsewhere. Pinsker wrote: *'The Jew was an uncanny apparition, and it was fear of this 'Jewish Ghost' that created prejudice against them. Civil and political emancipation was not sufficient to raise them in the estimation of other peoples. The only corrective was the creation of a Jewish nationality, of a people living on its own soil. The Jewish people –* Pinsker concluded – *have no fatherland of their own; they have no rallying point, no centre of gravity, no government of their own, and no accredited representatives. They are everywhere as guests and nowhere at home.'*

An Inspired Leader

On Wednesday, May 2, 1860, in a Jewish home in Budapest, proud new parents rejoiced at the birth of their new-born son. Their child, who they named Theodore Herzl, appears to have been the one chosen by God to bring the dry bones of Israel together again; and back to the land of Israel.

Theodore Herzl lived for only forty four years, yet for most of those years, Herzl dedicated his life to the awakening of the scattered remnant of the Jewish people from their second period of exile. At the time of his calling, their exclusion from their appointed home-land had lasted for 1,802 years.

Just before he died, Herzl made known the secret of his life's work. Herzl revealed that at the age of twelve the Messiah had appeared to him in a vision and commissioned Herzl to perform great wonders and deeds for His people. (As we shall see in other matters recalled in this book, Herzl's age at the time of his calling was duly significant). Twenty five years later (Herzl was thirty-seven) he arranged the First Zionist Congress which was held in Basel, Switzerland, and was a keynote speaker. After the Congress, and on the 3rd of September, 1897, Herzl wrote in his diary: *'Were I to sum up the Basle Congress in a word, it would be this, "At Basle I founded the Jewish State". 'If I said this out loud today, I would be answered by universal laughter. Perhaps in five years, **and certainly in fifty** [years], everyone will know it.'*

Seventeen years after the Congress the world was at war (1914). A direct result of the outcome of the First World War (some historians have said the First World War achieved nothing) was to allow Britain to take control of Palestine (1917). Thirty-one years later, (1948) Jewish people began to return freely to their original homeland. How did this happen?

As the war progressed, Britain's position became perilous as the tide of war began to move against her. Raw materials necessary for the manufacture of high explosives had become virtually unobtainable. Help, however, was on the horizon. Lord Balfour, a senior British politician, had a friend who taught chemistry at Manchester University and Balfour travelled to Manchester to ask his friend if he could help.

Balfour's friend set to work, and soon discovered a very simple method by which synthetic acetone could be procured from natural materials (which were readily available throughout Britain) and which could be used for the manufacture of high explosives.

Balfour's friend was the Jewish research chemist, Chaim Weizmann. The material Weizmann used to manufacture synthetic acetone was the seemingly harmless and inconspicuous horse chestnut. Robert Payne, author of *'The Splendor of Israel'* (1963), wrote: *'Dr. Weizmann set to work, devised a process of procuring acetone from horse chestnuts, and soon the factories were producing as much acetone as anyone could want.'*

Robert Payne was able to confirm this remarkable story when he wrote: *'Millions of horse chestnuts were gathered by children – and I was one of the children who collected the horse chestnuts!'*

By harnessing the potential of what was known by my school-friends and myself in the 1950s as conkers, the fortune of war began to turn in Britain's favor. When he was asked what reward he would like to receive from the British Government for making this simple, yet nation-saving discovery, Weizmann replied that he did not want anything for himself; however, Weizmann did say he would like Palestine to be given as a national homeland to his people, the Jewish people – which Britain now controlled!

The People of Israel

As a result (partly) of Weizmann's discovery, the Balfour Declaration (issued on 2nd November, 1917), stated Britain viewed with favor the establishment of a national homeland for the Jewish people in Palestine – an area Britain had just taken control of by having ousted Turkey in the process! Is it not remarkable that this land – known today as Israel – has its roots in a Jew who discovered that horse chestnuts could be used to make high explosives (to save Britain from defeat), and that these events took place just twenty years after Herzl's speech in 1897?

Following the First Zionist Congress (1897), Jewish people began to seriously consider how they might be able to return to their much-loved former homeland. Unfortunately, from 1917 and for the next thirty-one years, when the British government had the League of Nations mandate for administering Palestine, Britain actively opposed large scale Jewish emigration to Palestine. Jewish people would have to wait until the end of another world war for the opportunity – and a compelling incentive – for them to return to the land God had promised them. But sadly, it was from the *"Valley of Dry Bones"* they would eventually return.

A direct result of the suffering inflicted upon Jewish people during the time of the Second World War was there was no alternative but for them to return to the land God had promised them. In rejecting the plight of the Jews in Europe, a large part of the world had turned against them. But God had no intention of doing so, for they are a people who can trace their ancestry back to Abraham and the promises which God made with Abraham and his descendants.

Towards the end of the Second World War in Europe, U.S. President Franklin D. Roosevelt, asked Britain's Prime Minister Mr Winston Churchill, for suggestions about the war and how it should be remembered. In his reply to the American President, Prime Minister Churchill wrote: *'The Unnecessary War'*.

In Churchill's memoirs (*'THE SECOND WORLD WAR, Volume 1, The Gathering Storm'*), Churchill explained: *"There never was a war more easy to stop than that which has just wrecked what was left of the world from the previous struggle."* (i.e., The First World War).

The irony and tragedy of *'The Unnecessary War'* was that it resulted in an estimated fifty-five million people being killed. For the majority of those who died, Gentiles, they died because of the horror of war. For the Jews who died – nearly six million of them – most of them died because they were Jews. With hindsight, the events preceding the establishment of a nation state for the Jewish people in the Middle East are very perplexing; nevertheless, after nearly two millennia of persecution and separation from their home-land, the final outcome of the first and second world wars led directly to a modern-day miracle – the establishment of Israel.

The Stars of Heaven

In John's book of the revelation of Jesus Christ, John sees a vision of a dragon having seven heads and ten horns, with seven diadems on his heads. The dragon then drew with his tail: *'A third of the stars of heaven and <u>threw them to the earth</u>'* (Revelation 12:3–4).

It was not until I began to consider the twentieth century's history of the Jewish people that I sought to understand this scripture. Scientists have said that if a large asteroid collided with planet earth it could destroy the world as we know it. Can you imagine what would happen if a third of the stars of heaven collided with us? Not only is it not possible (the earth is not that big!), but such a cataclysmic event would destroy a large part of the Cosmos, if not the entire Cosmos. A literal happening may not be what this scripture is indicating.

As I began to think about this I asked: *"Does this sign have anything at all to do with the Jewish people?"* And so I turned to the Internet. Here I discovered that during the years 1938–1945 (1938 was the year Hitler began his war on Germany's Jews), one third of all the world's Jews were slaughtered – men, women and children were literally *thrown to the earth*. For those whose bodies were incinerated, their ashes were spread on fields to act as a fertilizer. For others, their bodies were buried in mass graves – which for many they had been forced to dig for themselves.

When recalling these not-so-long-ago events, I then remembered God's promise to His friend Abraham. *'Then He [God] brought Abraham outside and said, "Look now toward Heaven and count the stars if you are able to number them." And He said to him: "So shall your descendants be" '* (Genesis 15:5).

Could this (prophetic) vision in Revelation 12 about the stars of heaven, be a reference to the plight of the Jewish people in Europe during the years 1938–1945? Are there other scriptures which might support such a theory? Almost certainly there are, and just two may suffice. In Deuteronomy 1:10, we read: *"The Lord your God has multiplied you, and here you are today, as the stars of heaven in multitude."*

And in Hebrews: *'Therefore from one man [Abraham] and him as good as dead, were born as many as the stars in the sky in multitude – innumerable as the sand which is by the seashore'* (Hebrews 11:12).

The writer of the epistle to the Hebrews is stating that when Isaac was conceived, Abraham was as good as dead – because of his advanced years. This is not so dissimilar to the dry bones in the valley Ezekiel saw; bones in human terms which had no possibility of ever possessing life. For Abraham and his wife Sarah, it seemed impossible for them to have children, yet God enabled them to do so and Isaac's birth was in fulfilment of God's promise to Abraham. Isaac was Abraham's first star!

The evil nature of the Holocaust is one which resulted in immense pain for those who became its victims; for those who were so cruelly killed, but also for those who survived. What is so perplexing is apparently ordinary well-educated and sane people were willing to become executioners, and to murder (apparently without conscience) men, women and children.

Was it a case, as with the woman who was with child and who was in labor and pain to give birth (see Revelation 12:3–4), that as the fiery dragon who drew with his tail a third of the stars of heaven (the six million Jews who died), that those who carried out these horrific crimes were following Hitler – *acting like an animal's tail which always follows the animal* – in his hatred of the Jews?

Abraham's Yellow Stars

During the 1930s and the 1940s, for every Jew killed during the Holocaust, the majority of them went to their deaths wearing a yellow star. It was a symbol of hatred first introduced in the thirteenth century by those who thought of themselves as Christians, so they could identify and persecute Jewish people.

It has been estimated that during the Holocaust, 5,978,000 Jewish people died. According to the 1938 World Almanac, the worldwide population of Jewish people in 1938 was 16,588,259. Of course, neither of these two figures can be 100% accurate; nevertheless, information available for all to see suggests that during the years 1938–1945, one third of all Jewish people in the world (Abraham's stars) suffered a premature and violent death (as first recorded almost 2,000 years earlier in Revelation chapter twelve).

Rev. Leslie Hardman

On the 15th April, 1945, the Belsen concentration camp was liberated by British troops. The Rev. Leslie Hardman, MBE, a British chaplain and a Jew, was assigned to the first unit to enter Belsen. In his book, *'THE SURVIVORS – The Story of the Belsen Remnant'* (1958), Hardman describes the scene he witnessed as he entered the camp for the first time. *'Towards us came what seemed to me the remnants of a holocaust – a tottering mass of blackened skin and bones, held together somehow with filthy rags. "My God, the dead are walking" I cried aloud.'*

Is it possible this horrific scene which Rev. Hardman witnessed as he first walked into Belsen, was in fact part of the scene God had revealed to His servant Ezekiel, more than 2,500 years earlier?

'Therefore prophesy and say to them, "Thus says the LORD GOD: Behold, O My people, I will open your graves and cause you to come up from your graves, and bring you into the land of Israel. Then you shall know that I am the LORD, when I have opened your graves, O My people, and brought you up from your

graves. I will put My Spirit in you, and you shall live, and I will place you in your own land. Then you shall know that I, the LORD, have spoken it and performed it, says the LORD"' (Ezekiel 37:12–14).

When Rev. Hardman saw a small group of those who had not died – although many of them died later – and he cried out: *"My God, the dead are walking!"* later he wrote in his diary: *'But I did not recognize my voice.'* Why did Rev. Hardman fail to recognize his voice? Was it because his words were inspired?

Charles Haddon Spurgeon

Today we can recall these times of recent history as the testimonies and the images are still with us. For those who lived in the nineteenth century, it was entirely different; the events I have described had not yet taken place.

In 1864, Charles Haddon Spurgeon, when preaching on the subject of Ezekiel's vision of the valley of dry bones, said: *"Israel is now blotted out from the map of nations; her sons are scattered far and wide; her daughters mourn beside all the rivers of the earth. Her sacred song is hushed; no king reigns in Jerusalem; she bringeth forth no governors among her tribes. But she is to be restored; she is to be restored, 'As from the dead'."*

"When her own sons have given up all hope of her, then is God to appear for her. She is to be re-

organized; her scattered bones are to be brought together. There will be a native government again; there will again be the form of a body politic; a state shall be incorporated and a king shall reign."

"Israel has now become alienated from her own land. Her sons, though they can never forget the sacred dust of Palestine, yet die at a hopeless distance from her consecrated shores. But it shall not be so forever, for her sons shall again rejoice in her; her land shall be called Beulah, for as a young man marrieth a virgin, so shall her sons marry her. 'I will place you in your own land' is God's promise to them."

In his time (and even today) Spurgeon was considered to have been an exceptional Bible teacher; therefore, I quote what Spurgeon went on to say concerning the spiritual conversion of the Jewish people:

"Looking at this matter, we are very apt to say: How can these things be? How can the Jews be converted to Christ? How can they be made into a nation? Truly, the case is quite as hopeless as that of the bones in the valley! How shall they cease from worldliness, or renounce their constant pursuit of riches? How shall they be weaned from their bigoted attachment to their Talmudic traditions? How shall they be lifted up out of that hardness of heart which makes them hate the Messiah of Nazareth, their Lord and King? How can these things be? The prophet does not say it cannot be; his unbelief is not so great

as that, but at the same time, he scarcely ventures to think that it can ever be possible. He very wisely, however, puts back the question upon his God – Lord God, thou knowest."

Isaiah Chapter Six

On 13th October, 2011, while reading in the book of Isaiah, the word Holocaust seized my attention. But why had this word suddenly sprung itself upon me; it was not included in my reading. At the time I had no idea, but I was aware the whisper I had sensed was one not to be ignored, and so I continued reading.

In the sixth chapter of Isaiah, we read of a time-related event that would eventually affect both the land of Israel and God's people. God informed Isaiah that Israel's cities would one day be: *"Laid waste and without inhabitant, the houses are without a man, the land is utterly desolate, the LORD has removed men far away, and the forsaken places are many in the midst of the land"* (Isaiah 6:11–12). This prophecy describes the land of Israel as being a wasteland.

This description of Israel's cities and its land is very similar to the description found in Ezekiel 36:4. It is also clear that this description is very similar to a United Nations report concerning Palestine which was published in September 1947.

In 1947, prior to Israel being declared a new an independent country, a United Nations commissioned report stated that Palestine was: *'Disease-ridden, under-developed, poverty stricken; it had the scantiest facilities for education, virtually no industry and an indifferent agricultural regime. Internally, it was given to lawlessness and it was open to the predatory attention of nomad bands from the desert.'*

These three independent reports, the first two written two-and-a-half millennia ago, the third as recently as September 1947, are uncannily similar in their detail. Yet despite these very detailed descriptions of an abandoned and poverty stricken land, God informed Isaiah: *"But yet a tenth will be in it, and will return and be for consuming"* (Isaiah 6:13). *'Consuming'* can also mean: *'Burning'*. So how does the Holocaust fit within the description of Isaiah chapter six?

Knowing the word Holocaust means *'Burnt Offering'*, and that the majority of the victims of the Holocaust had been consumed (burnt) in the Nazi's crematoria, I paused to consider: Did God inform Isaiah about this horrific episode experienced by His people in Europe during the years 1933 to 1945? (1933 was the year when Hitler came to power). And was the tenth identified in Isaiah 6:13, the proportion of God's people who would be saved from the Holocaust, or is there another explanation for God's revelation to His servant Isaiah?

Before we examine this passage in Isaiah, it's worth remembering that the term a tenth as being a remnant of God's people is one that is also referred to in the book of Amos. Although the following statement may appear at first sight to be of minor importance, it ends with a ringing assurance which eclipses many other well-known passages.

'Hear this word which I take up against you, a lamentation, O house of Israel: The virgin of Israel has fallen; she will rise no more. She lies forsaken on her land; there is no one to raise her up. For thus says the LORD GOD: "The city that goes out by a thousand shall have a hundred left, and that which goes out by a hundred shall have ten left to the house of Israel." For thus says the LORD to the house of Israel: "Seek Me and live"' (Amos 5:1–4).

God's messages, both to Isaiah and to Amos, appear to confirm that reference to a remnant of a tenth of God's people is not an isolated occurrence. Also, God's promise to Israel that if they seek God they will *'Live'*, is repeated in this chapter in Amos no less than three times – verses 4, 6 and 14. When taking note of God's yearning for His people, my thoughts regarding the preserving of a tenth took me back to Theodore Herzl who had arranged the First Zionist Congress in Basle, Switzerland. The date Herzl wrote up his report about what had taken place at the Congress was the 3rd September, 1897.

Twenty years later, on the 9th December 1917, the mayor of Jerusalem, Hussein Husseini, surrendered

Jerusalem to British forces. Was it a co-incidence – or a God-incident – that the surrender of Jerusalem took place at *'Hanukkah'*, the time in the Jewish calendar when a number of biblical scholars believe Jesus was conceived? (In my book, *'Hebrew Foundations of the Christian Faith'*, I have written about the importance of Hanukkah and how this ancient Jewish festival is likely to be linked to the conception of Jesus). When taking note of these two dates, it is prudent to see that God's plans for His people frequently link historical detail with particular moments in time; therefore, in biblical terms (and by definition), time can often be looked-upon as being holy.

Thirty years later, in September 1947, the United Nations Special Committee On Palestine (UNSCOP) issued their report (the same report I referred to earlier) about how Palestine should be divided between its Jewish and Arab inhabitants. A few weeks later the United Nations General Assembly voted in favour of UNSCOP's recommendation – to establish a Jewish and an Arab homeland in Palestine. Their recommendation was in line with Britain's 1917 Balfour Declaration.

For over two thousand years the Jewish homeland had been dominated by a succession of foreign powers – but each in turn had neglected it. Then, in 1947, the status of part of Palestine was about to change, to become Israel. The date UNSCOP published their report (I have a copy), was the 3rd September 1947. It was fifty years to the day from when Herzl had noted in his diary that Palestine would become: *'If not in five years, yet within fifty years, a Jewish State –* [and] *everyone will know it.'* Herzl's margin of error (although he never knew it), was an incredible 0.00%!

The 3rd September is important for a third reason, for it was on this day in 1939 that Britain, who at the time had the League of Nations mandate to administer Palestine, declared war on Germany. <u>*Exactly eight years later*</u>, on the 3rd September 1947 – in Hebrew, eight is a sign of regeneration, the start of a new era or order – was when UNSCOP published their report that Israel should be restored. Nine months later (the gestation period for the human embryo), was when Israel's birth took place.

Theodor Herzl, who inspired the restoration of Israel, knew from his experience as a father that new life does not begin when a child emerges from the womb, but life begins from the day a child is conceived. Thus when UNSCOP made known their recommendation/ declaration that Israel should again be established in its original homeland, the news was announced by the world's representatives. The announcement of Israel's day of conception came fifty years to the day from when Herzl had made his prediction. In Hebrew understanding, fifty years is a period which represents a time of jubilee, or deliverance. After fifty years it is the time to rest. After so much pain and suffering, this was precisely what the Jewish people were in need of.

Nine months later, on the 14th May, 1948, following a period of intense pain for the Jewish people, they and their land – the two who had been persecuted and neglected for nearly 2,000 years – became Israel. It was the right time for Israel's birth to take place.

The estimated number of Jewish people who died in the Holocaust is often quoted as six million. When UNSCOP published its report, UNSCOP estimated that the number of Jews living in Palestine in 1946 – a year after the war in Europe ended – was 608,225. This was one tenth of the number of those who had died. Many of those who had survived the Holocaust (and those who had fled from Germany in the 1930s when the fear of death was becoming a real threat, fled to British-controlled Palestine in order to escape persecution. They did so because there was nowhere else for them to go.

With the threat of annihilation hanging over them, like the *'Sword of Damocles'*, who could blame them for fleeing to Palestine, their promised and much-loved homeland?

2,500 years ago, God informed Isaiah: *"Yet a tenth will be in it, and will return and be for consuming [burning]"* (Isaiah 6:13). The margin of error, based on those who had died in the Holocaust, versus those living in what at the time was still Palestine and who had escaped the burning, was 0.1%. In May 1945, when the war in Europe ended, the margin of error would have been less than 0.1%, for the estimate of the number of Jews living in Palestine was based on a census taken in 1946.

What I have also discovered that is amazing, is that in 1947 the temporary offices of the United Nations from where UNSCOP prepared its report was located on the outskirts of New York in an area known as *'Lake Success'* – but there is no lake there!

On the 1st March, 2012, I wrote to a friend about Isaiah 6:13 and presented him with my explanation of how I understood this important passage – the one which states the Lord will preserve a tenth. My friend kindly replied and asked the following question:

'David, I confess to being mystified by the reference to those who suffered in the Holocaust, versus those who formed the nation of Israel, and their correlation with the statement in Isaiah. It appears you are saying that although six million Jews perished in the Holocaust, the 600,000 will, to fit in with Isaiah, also be for consuming! Perhaps this is not what you intended to say, but that is how I have perceived it.'

My friend's reply was entirely valid, because it meant I needed to consider this passage again. Isaiah six is an important chapter, because it is when Isaiah saw: *'The Lord sitting on a throne, high and lifted up, and the train of His robe filled the temple'* (Isaiah 6:1). Dare I suggest such experiences are quite rare?

What is also interesting is that although Isaiah was informed of God's warning, it appears Isaiah – yes, willing to deliver God's message, *"Here am I! Send me."* – was not the one intended to bring this message to God's people. There is no mention in the book of Isaiah that he did so. However, we do know that Jesus told His disciples that this message was a prophecy intended for a future generation – His generation. Matthew 13:14–15 is a repeat of Isaiah 6:9–10.

Immediately after the detail about God's warning as recorded by Isaiah (but given to Israel by Jesus), we read that Isaiah then asked: *"Lord, how long?"* His reply was: *"Until the cities are laid waste and without inhabitant, the houses are without a man and the land is utterly desolate, the Lord has removed men far away and the forsaken places are many in the midst of the land"* (Isaiah 6:11–12).

God's warning could not have taken place until *underline*after*underline* Jesus had repeated this warning; which He did during His time of ministry. Historically, we now know the consequences of this prophecy were spread over a period of approximately 1,800 years; from shortly after Jesus had repeated this prophecy, to the year 1864 when Spurgeon preached his famous sermon – thus precipitating/anticipating the return of the Jewish people. This prophecy then culminated in the two most deadliest of wars in human history – the first and second world wars – during which tens of millions of people, both Jews and Gentiles, perished.

The People of Israel

The Reverend Leslie Hardman conducting his first funeral service at the Belsen concentration camp. The mass-grave Rev. Hardman is facing contained five thousand bodies.

It was at Belsen Rev. Hardman recorded in his diary when he first entered the camp: *'Towards us came what seemed to me the remnants of a holocaust – a tottering mass of blackened skin and bones, held together somehow with filthy rags. "My God, the dead are walking" I cried aloud.'*

Later, after he had time to reflect on what he had said, Rev. Hardman wrote: *'I did not recognize my voice.'*

****

Photograph courtesy of the Imperial War Museum, London (BU4269). Used with permission.

ACRIMONY – BITTERNESS

In early 1940, German forces invaded Denmark and Norway. Having subjugated these two sovereign nations, Hitler then turned his attention to attack Holland, Belgium and France. In a matter of weeks, Hitler's troops had defeated five nations. What has mystified historians is why Hitler withheld his forces and allowed Britain to evacuate a third of a million troops from the beaches at Dunkirk, thus enabling them to fight another day. We know King George VI called for a national day of prayer for the troops to be safely evacuated, and this is the most likely reason why so many soldiers were rescued. Their rescuers were mostly civilians in small boats (the *'small'* being used to bring about a big effect), as was the case when Jesus used a boy's lunch to feed five thousand people. God's method is often to use small beginnings – or insignificant people – for His greater purposes.

Following the conquest of five nations, many believed Britain was the next to be defeated. Britain was only twenty miles from mainland Europe and it was only a matter of time before an invasion could take place. First, however, Hitler had to secure aerial superiority, but in this he failed, because of the outcome of the Battle of Britain – as Churchill confirmed on the 21st of August 1940: *"Never in the field of human conflict was so much owed by so many to so few."*

Acrimony - Bitterness

Had Hitler invaded Britain, Britain's Jews, including the many thousands of Jewish children who had fled from Austria, Czechoslovakia and Germany on the kinder transports prior to the war, they also would have become victims of the Holocaust.

Hitler's next move was to plan his invasion of Soviet Russia, thereby annulling Germany's non-aggression pact which the two countries had signed on the 23rd of August, 1939. By early 1941, German forces were being made ready to invade Russia, an invasion which would enable Hitler's plan for the liquidation of Russia's Jews to take place. At the same time, Italy's Mussolini, who was jealous of Hitler's victories in northern Europe, extended his territorial ambitions in the Balkans by invading Greece. His troops, however, were overwhelmed by Grecian forces and forced back into Albania.

Hitler, although annoyed by his allies' incompetence, was obliged to come to Mussolini's rescue, and in so doing moved large sections of his forces south, knowing it would lead to a delay in carrying out *'Operation Barbarossa'* – his invasion of Russia. As a result of Germany's involvement in the Balkans, the invasion of Russia was delayed from May 1941 to late June 1941. A number of historians, such as Sir John Keegan and Richard Overy, have said that the delay in carrying out *'Operation Barbarossa'* was a significant factor in Germany's ultimate failure to defeat Russia.

By the end of May 1941, Greece and the island of Crete had fallen victim to German forces. Hitler's hatred of the Jews, which included the large Jewish population in Thessalonica (Saloniki), meant that the decision was taken to confine the Jews to a Ghetto. During March 1943, in freight trains carrying two thousand Jews apiece, nearly 50,000 Jews from Thessalonica were taken to the death camps at Auschwitz-Birkenau and Treblinka to be killed.

It was in these two camps the majority of the Jews from Greece were gassed and their bodies incinerated. At the end of the war, it became known that from Greece alone, at least 54,000 Jews had been murdered. As the slaughter of Europe's Jews continued, what hope was there for those Jews who were then living in Palestine?

Meanwhile, as these things were happening in the northern regions of the Mediterranean Sea, General Rommel, known as the *'Desert Fox'*, commander of Germany's Afrika Korps, began his advance across North Africa. By the end of July 1942, German troops were positioned only seventy miles from Alexandria, with Palestine (as the promised land was then called) not far away.

With German forces based on the island of Crete and approaching Egypt along the coast road of North Africa, and German troops engaged in an offensive to defeat Stalingrad and so open a route south over the

Caucasus mountains to enter the Middle East via Turkey and Syria, prospects for the Jews in Palestine were becoming life-threatening – they must have been wondering if they were safe from Hitler's minions? What if they, like their brothers and sisters in Europe, were to become victims of Nazi hatred; what would happen to them? For those who had sought refuge in Palestine, they were aware they were not immune to persecution. In June 1941, the cities of Haifa and Tel Aviv had been bombed by Vichy forces based in Syria which had resulted in many civilian casualties.

I am sure throughout the years of the Second World War a number of Jewish people may have thought they had escaped persecution. Towards the end of 1944, among the many Jews then living in Hungary, relatively few of them had been transported by train to the Nazi death camps. With Russian forces advancing rapidly from the east, and allied forces advancing from the west, it was only a matter of time before they, too, would be safe. It was not to be, and in the final stages of the war tens of thousands of Hungarian Jews were transported by train to the death camps and murdered.

Trees and their Roots

At this point, I would like to include an illustration.

A few years ago a retired person I once worked for asked me to cut down three large trees. With the help of a chain saw the work was not difficult; and when it came to cutting up the trees after they had been felled, once again, the task was quite straight-forward. The difficulty arises when trying to remove the stumps and their roots. Without the right type of equipment it is nearly impossible for one person to remove the roots of a large tree. But why have I recalled such detail? It is because it is related to Isaiah 6:13 and the tenth of God's people who were destined to return and be for consuming (for burning).

For Jewish people then living in Palestine, many of them escapees from Germany, this was what many were now considering as their most likely destiny as they witnessed hostile forces surrounding them.

One might say (and we now know this to be true), this was a sincerely held conviction: *"If Hitler invades Palestine, we're finished."* For those who had only recently fled from Europe, it must have seemed there was nowhere where they could find safety. They knew other countries, including Britain, had rejected them; therefore, where could they escape to?

In 1942 and in Palestine, with hundreds of thousands of German troops surrounding them, Jewish people were aware they might so easily end their lives in Hitler's crematoria. *"Are we about to become victims of the burning of Jewish people?"* was what many were beginning to ask themselves. With Hitler's forces seemingly invincible, death must have seemed a real threat for the majority of them. However, let us now consider the second part of Isaiah 6:13. It reads as follows: *"As a terebinth tree or as an oak, whose stump remains when it is cut down. So the holy seed shall be its stump."* In biblical terms, the terebinth tree and the oak tree are known for their strength and longevity.

Israel the Tree

The metaphor of the tree is one used by Isaiah when told to record a prophetic message – only part of which was quoted by Jesus in a synagogue in Nazareth. When Jesus stood to read, according to His custom, He was handed the book of the prophet Isaiah. Having opened the book, He found the place where it was written: *"The Spirit of the LORD is upon Me, because He has anointed Me to preach the gospel to the poor; He has sent Me to heal the brokenhearted, to proclaim liberty to the captives and recovery of sight to the blind, to set at liberty those who are oppressed; to proclaim the acceptable year of the LORD..."* (Luke 4:18–19). Surprisingly, instead of continuing, Jesus stopped in mid-sentence. Jesus then closed the book, gave it back to the attendant, and sat down. Jesus then said: *"Today, this scripture is fulfilled in your hearing"* (Luke 4:21).

The words Jesus quoted were about Himself. If Jesus had continued to read, He would have said: *"...and the day of vengeance of our God; to comfort all who mourn, to console those who mourn in Zion, to give them beauty for ashes, the oil of joy for mourning, the garment of praise for the spirit of heaviness; that they may be called trees of righteousness, the planting of the LORD that He may be glorified"* (Isaiah 61:2–3).

Why did Jesus stop half-way in His quote of this prophecy? Was it because it refers to two periods of time? The first period was certainly applicable to His first coming – He said so. The second period appears to refer to a time of God's mercy towards Israel. If this is true, the words which follow are also of great importance – because only then: *'And they shall rebuild the old ruins, they shall raise up the former desolations, and they shall repair the ruined cities, the desolations of many generations'* (Isaiah 61:4).

Regarding this synopsis, was Israel told a second time about this future acrimonious event? Indeed she was, and the metaphor of the tree was again used; this time by John the Baptist who, according to Jesus, was the greatest prophet of all time (Matthew 11:11). John the Baptist warned his fellow countrymen: *"Do not think to say to yourselves, 'We have Abraham as our father.' For I say to you that God is able to raise up children to Abraham from these stones.* ***And even now the axe is laid to the root of the trees. Therefore every tree which does not bear good fruit is cut down and thrown into the fire"*** (Matthew 3:9–10). As John the Baptist said, eventually it took place. Israel was cut down by the Romans in 70 CE.

Notwithstanding these events, Israel's stump and its roots have always remained. There has always been a Jewish presence in God's land. The remarkable thing about the Jews is that throughout the centuries of being persecuted and dispersed, when they had no homeland like other people groups, nevertheless, they retained their identity as a nation – albeit in exile. This has never happened to any other people group.

Using the tree metaphor, God's promise continues: *"They shall build houses and inhabit them; they shall plant vineyards and eat their fruit. They shall not build and another inhabit; they shall not plant and another eat; for as the days of a <u>tree</u>, so shall be the days of My people, and My elect shall long enjoy the work of their hands."* (Isaiah 65:21–22).

Incredibly, in this our generation, we have seen the fulfilment of this promise which was given to Isaiah regarding God's people Israel. The apostle Paul also confirmed this would one-day happen, when he described how the natural branches, the Jewish people, would be grafted in again into their own olive tree (Romans 11:24).

During the years 1938–1945, for Jews in much of Europe and elsewhere, there were few places where they could be assured of safety. In Germany and the lands Germany had occupied, Jews were being forced into slavery and into Hitler's *'Final Solution'* – death to be followed by cremation. Therefore, surely, if

German forces had reached Palestine (and in late 1942 they were in close proximity), the remnant, the stump, the approximately 600,000 Jewish people who God in His wisdom had planted in His land (as it says in Isaiah 61:3 when referring to the survival of Jewish people, *"The planting of the LORD that He may be glorified"*), they also would have perished.

Thankfully, they were kept safe, because God had promised Isaiah that the stump, the remnant of God's people joined to the land in which they had been planted, although intended for consuming, they would remain secure. Equally important, they would be kept alive, for it was God who prevented their murder from taking place.

It must be horrific to see your loved-ones murdered and their bodies incinerated into ashes. However, to realize you are likely to be death's next victim, such fear must be akin to that felt by those who had already been killed. I believe that at the time for Jews then living in Palestine, the fear of them being consumed was what must have concerned them. The fact, however, they were the *'holy seed'* (Ezra 9:2), and *'Abraham's seed'* (Luke 1:55), was their assurance that God would not allow His promise to Isaiah, and thus to Israel, to fail. Israel today is a testimony to the nations of God honoring His historic commitment.

Some, like my friend who wrote to me, may have read from God's message to Isaiah (6:13), confirmation that the remnant would be consumed. Was this possible? Indeed it was, for early twenty-first century research by Martin Cuppers from the University of Berlin, and Klaus-Michael Mallmann from the University of Ludwigsburg, has led to material being discovered indicating how the Nazis were planning to murder all the Jews in the countries of the Middle East, had they succeeded in suppressing the region. There is no doubt for the Jews then living in Palestine the vast majority of them would have perished.

Moses, Gideon and Rees Howells

God often chooses the unlikeliest of his people for his greater purposes. For example: Moses who said he was not eloquent (Exodus 4:10), and Gideon who said he was the least in his father's house (Judges 6:15). In times of a crisis, such as war, this is especially so. On the 4th of July 1942, Rees Howells, the Principle of the Bible College of Wales, assembled his staff and his students and asked them to pray.

Prior to engaging in prayer, Mr. Howells said to them: *'Unless God will intervene on behalf of Palestine, there will be no safety there for the Jews. These Bible lands must be protected, because it is to these lands the Saviour will come back. If I had a choice today, I would say to God, "Take all I have, but preserve Palestine." We want to say to God today, "Unless there is a special reason for Egypt to fall, don't let Alexandria be taken, but give Rommel a setback. Can*

I carry the same burden today for Alexandria as I would if Swansea were being attacked?' Mr. Howells, an intercessor in times of spiritual warfare, knew that prayer was the key to victory. The following day Mr. Howells wrote: *'I thought he* [Rommel] *might be allowed to take Egypt, but now I know he will never take Egypt – neither Alexandria nor Cairo will fall.'*

One from a City, Two from a Family

There may be some who although they believe in the Bible, say there is no (written) evidence God intended Israel to return to the global scene. Such evidence, if it does exist, must be carefully examined to correct any unintentional misunderstanding of the prospect of the Jewish people's return to their former homeland.

Together with the examination of historical material, it is appropriate to consider a promise given by God through Jeremiah by reviewing two accounts of personal survival which arose from the aftermath of the Holocaust.

Ruth Elias

Ruth Elias, a Jewess, was born and grew-up with her family in the Moravian city of Ostrava. On 2nd April 1942, Ruth and her family were sent to the ghetto at Thereisienstadt. Later in the war, Ruth was sent to the concentration camp at Ravensbruck, then to the death camp at Auschwitz. Finally, Ruth was sent to the slave-labour camp at Buchenwald.

Miraculously Ruth survived Hitler's attempt to destroy Europe's Jews. Sadly, however, the rest of her family perished. During the four years after the war, Ruth's reply to those who enquired about her family was: *"They've probably all been gassed."*

Ruth was the only survivor of her very large family, the story of which she describes in her book *'Triumph of Hope'*. When Ruth returned to her home city she was treated as a stranger, and so for Ruth there was no longer a reason for her to stay in Czechoslovakia. On the 1st April, 1949, Ruth boarded a train in Prague to travel to her chosen destination – Israel. Ruth had come to the conclusion that there was no future for her if she remained in her former homeland. For Ruth, it was time for her to go up to Zion.

Rabbi Hugo Gryn

Rabbi Hugo Gryn was born in Berehovo on the 25th June, 1930. In his book *'Chasing Shadows'*, Rabbi Gryn provides a description of himself. *'A man from Berehovo arrives at the gates of heaven. "Before you can enter," says the guardian angel, "you have to tell us the story of your life." "Well," the man replies, "I was born in the Austro-Hungarian Empire to decent and God-fearing parents, received my education in Czechoslovakia and started to work as an apprentice in Hungary. For a time I also worked in Germany, but I raised my own family and did most of my life's work in the Soviet Union." The angel was impressed, "You certainly travelled and moved about a great deal."* "*Oh, no,*" *the man protested,* "*I never left Berehovo!"*

Rabbi Gryn was still a teenager when the Second World War in Europe ended, and was a survivor of Auschwitz and numerous other slave labour camps. Hugo and his mother were the only two members of their family to have survived the war – his father died in his arms just a few days after the war ended.

After the war, Hugo rarely spoke about his family's ordeal. It was not until January 1978, over thirty years after the war in Europe had ended, that Hugo spoke for the first time publicly about his sufferings in the Nazi death camps. In Auschwitz, Hugo became a number – 80,494.

Recalling his time spent in the Auschwitz death-camp, Hugo wrote in his memoirs: *'I found God in this living hell.'* Hugo continued: *'God, the God of Abraham, could not abandon me; I could only abandon God. I believe that God was there Himself – violated and blasphemed. The real question is: "Where was man in Auschwitz?"'*

If you know anything about Hitler's obsession to destroy the Jews, then you will know that family losses like those experienced by Ruth and Hugo were not uncommon for those who survived the war. For some, they were the only Jewish person from a particular town or city to have survived – as in Ruth's case. For others, only two members from a family were saved – as in Rabbi Hugo Gryn's case. But what do these comparatively recent events have to do with the prophet Jeremiah?

The answer is given in Jeremiah 3:11–14.

'Then the LORD said to me, "Backsliding Israel has shown herself more righteous than treacherous Judah. Go and proclaim these words toward the north and say: 'Return backsliding Israel', says the LORD; 'I will not cause My anger to fall on you. For I am merciful', says the LORD; 'I will not remain angry forever. Only acknowledge your iniquity that you have transgressed against the LORD your God, and have scattered your charms to alien deities under every green tree, and you have not obeyed My voice', says the LORD. 'Return, O backsliding children', says the LORD; 'for I am married to you. I will take you, <u>one from a city</u>, and <u>two from a family</u> and I will bring you to Zion'."

In extraordinary detail, God informed Jeremiah of how from a worldwide dispersion of the Jews, God would bring His people back to the land of Israel. Jeremiah was told of these events six hundred years before the second exile of the Jews commenced.

For survivors such as Ruth Elias, the only Jewish person (from a city) to have survived, or when two from a family were saved, such as Hugo Gryn and his mother, their deliverance from the Holocaust was in fulfilment of God's promise to Jeremiah. Only God could have known about these survivors, and because He knew, He was able to tell His servant Jeremiah to write about them and to describe their eventual return to the land to which He would restore them.

For those who survived the trauma of the Holocaust and who returned to their former homeland – together with the Jewish remnant, the tenth – they immediately set about working for its restoration and prosperity. The presence of the Jewish people and the way they have transformed the land of Israel into a vibrant and prosperous nation, illustrates clearly how the land and its people – and their connection to their Messiah – are a light to the nations as God originally intended.

'And now the LORD says, who formed Me from the womb to be His Servant, to bring Jacob back to Him, so that Israel is gathered to Him (For I shall be glorious in the eyes of the LORD, and My God shall be My strength), indeed He says, "Is it too small a thing that You should be My Servant to raise up the tribes of Jacob, and to restore the preserved ones of Israel; I will also give You as a light to the Gentiles, that You should be My salvation to the ends of the earth" (Isaiah 49:5–6). Here, Jesus is included.

Isaiah also explains why God has caused His people to return to the land He gave to their forefathers.

Acrimony - Bitterness

'Break forth into joy, sing together, you waste places of Jerusalem! For the LORD has comforted His people, He has redeemed Jerusalem. The Lord has made bare His holy arm in the eyes of all the nations; and all the ends of the earth shall see the salvation of our God (Isaiah 52:9–10).

From the time when Israel was once again restored as a nation – that the Jewish people might: *"Seek Me* [God] *and live." "Seek the LORD and live." "Seek good and not evil, that you may live."* (Amos 5:4, 6 & 14) – the *'GOOD NEWS'* of Jesus has now reached the ends of the earth, to the Gentile nations, for God is redeeming Jerusalem.

Who would have thought, during the first half of the 1940s, that after such a bitter experience, the Jewish people would be restored to their beloved homeland? Most would not; however, God knew.

The breath of resurrection life has so clearly entered the valley which Ezekiel foresaw in his remarkable vision, that of *'The Valley of Dry Bones'*. And if for any reason you may doubt this has been God's work, then I recommend you board a plane and visit Israel. And while you are there, make sure you visit some of the Messianic communities which exist throughout Israel. I know you will be greatly encouraged.

As we draw near to the end of this section – and as we remember the plight and sorrow of the Jewish people during the years of their extended exile and of their restoration to the promised land – the following words from Psalm 124 seem, to me, as the most appropriate.

"If it had not been the LORD who was on our side," Let Israel now say – "If it was not the LORD who was on our side, when men rose up against us, then they would have swallowed us alive, when their wrath was kindled against us; then the waters would have overwhelmed us, the stream would have gone over our soul; then the swollen waters would have gone over our soul." Blessed be the LORD, who has not given us as prey to their teeth. Our soul has escaped as a bird from the snare of the fowlers; the snare is broken, and we have escaped. Our help is in the name of the LORD, who made heaven and earth.'

Christians United For Israel

Christians United For Israel (UK) is an organisation dedicated to asking Christians to stand with Israel. In a leaflet they have produced for why Christians should support Israel, they list a number of reasons for why this is important – including a reminder that God has promised to bless those who bless Israel.

With the kind permission of its Executive Director, Des Starritt, I list below ten reasons why they say Christians should stand with Israel.

1. Other nations were created by an act of men. Israel was created by an act of God.

2. Standing with Israel is standing against anti-Semitism.

3. The Jewish people have an historic right to the land of Israel.

4. Israel is the safest place for Christians to live in the Middle East.

5. The restoration of Israel to the Jewish people was an integral part of teaching in the Church in Britain for centuries.

6. Israel is the only true democracy in the Middle East.

7. Israeli innovation is saving and improving lives around the world.

8. Israel was chosen by God to implement His plan of Salvation – to Jews first, then to Gentiles (Romans 1:16).

9. The rebirth of modern-day Israel is a fulfilment of Bible prophecy.

10. Israel is a Bible issue not a political issue.

****

CAN A NATION BE BORN IN A DAY?

Many years ago I was told that if you examined every leaf from every tree you would never find two which were identical. The same is true of people; each life is unique. For example, God said to Jeremiah: *"Before I formed you in the womb I knew you; before you were born I sanctified you; I ordained you a prophet to the nations"* (Jeremiah 1:5).

From Ecclesiastes we are reminded there is a time for every purpose under heaven. After this introduction, there are listed twenty eight events which are related to time – such as: *'A time to be born and a time to die'* (3:2). Other events in the Bible are described as *'Appointed Times'*, and examples of these include Israel's seven annual festivals. Here, however, we are considering the Jewish people, their restoration to the promised land, and its significance.

Zechariah (like Jeremiah) was a man with whom God shared His concern for Israel. In Zechariah, chapters twelve and thirteen, ten statements are listed which state certain things will one day take place, and that when they do, they will take place at the same time. The introduction to each of these statements includes these words: *"In that day..."*. Some of the future things included in chapter twelve are: *"In that day the*

LORD will defend the inhabitants of Jerusalem; the one who is feeble among them in that day shall be like David, and the house of David shall be like God, like the Angel of the LORD before them. It shall be in that day that I will seek to destroy all the nations that come against Jerusalem. And I will pour on the house of David and on the inhabitants of Jerusalem the Spirit of grace and supplication; then they will look on Me [Jesus] whom they pierced. Yes, they will mourn for Him as one mourns for his only son, and grieve for Him as one grieves for a firstborn" (Zechariah 12:8–10).

Verse ten clearly refers to when Jesus comes a second time, and the Jewish people will receive Him as their Messiah. It is something the majority of them failed to do when He came the first time. And when they do receive Him, they will call on God's name. His response will be: *"This is My people"* and each one will say, *"The LORD is my God"* (Zechariah 13:9).

Two Exiles

It is helpful to recall that Moses was not the only one to warn Israel of two exiles. Isaiah also warned Israel, and he did so using the words God gave to him. *"For she has received from the LORD's hand double for all her sins"* (Isaiah 40:2). The word double can also mean twice, yet despite this, God promised Ezekiel He would restore Israel. *"For I will take you from among the nations, gather you out of all countries, and bring you into your own land. Then I will sprinkle clean water on you, and you shall be clean; I will cleanse you from all your filthiness and from all your idols. I will give you a new heart and put a new spirit within you; I will take the heart of stone out of your flesh and give you a heart of flesh. I will put My Spirit within you and cause you to walk in My statutes, and you will keep My judgments and do them. Then you shall dwell in the land that I gave to your fathers; and you shall be My people, and I will be your God. I will deliver you from all your uncleannesses"* (Ezekiel 36:24–29).

Until now I have recalled mainly Old Testament scriptures about the Jewish people's restoration to the promised land; however, as well as including these scriptures, did Jesus ever refer to some of these more recent events; events which continue to influence acts of anti-Semitism and defiance throughout the Gentile world? As we have seen, it has always been God's intention that the Jewish Diaspora was to be restored to the promised land in accordance with His covenant with Abraham, and not to remain as dry bones in the nations to which they had been scattered.

Because this is so important, did Jesus say (or do) anything about Israel's separation and restoration to the promised land? Surely, Jesus must have known about these things and would not have remained silent knowing that Israel's future and the climax of the ages would one day depend on it?

Can a Nation be Born in a Day?

We know that in His teaching Jesus used illustrations, because although the people had eyes to see, they could not see, they had ears to hear, but they could not hear or understand (Isaiah 6:9–10). However, to His disciples, Jesus said: *"Blessed are your eyes for they see, and your ears for they hear"* (Matthew 13:10–16). To understand the parables and the miracles Jesus performed is a blessing – for they symbolize meaning.

This, therefore, brings us to where we can now take some of these Old Testament scriptures, see how they are linked to New Testament scriptures, and see how the two are related. In doing so, first we will look at two events in the life of Jesus which took place on the same day and which apply to the atonement of the land of Israel (Ezekiel 36) and the restoration of the Jewish people (Ezekiel 37). The involvement of Jesus in these two events is featured first in the synoptic gospels. After we have considered these two events, or *'signs'*, we will then move to consider a third event in John's Gospel. Each of these three events appears to refer unequivocally to a promise once made by God with His servant Moses: *"Rejoice, O Gentiles, with His people; for He will avenge the blood of His servants, and render vengeance to His adversaries;* ***He will provide atonement for His land and His people.***" (Deuteronomy 32:43).

Before we proceed, please note from the last chapter in Isaiah the following declaration. This is where God compares Israel to a mother giving birth.

"Before she was in labor, she gave birth; before her pain came, she delivered a male child. Who has heard such a thing? Who has seen such things? **Shall the earth be made to give birth in one day? Or shall a nation be born at once?** *For as soon as Zion was in labor, she gave birth to her children. Shall I bring to the time of birth, and not cause delivery?" says the LORD. "Shall I who cause delivery shut up the womb?" says your God. "Rejoice with Jerusalem, and be glad with her, all you who love her. Rejoice for joy with her, all you who mourn for her; that you may feed and be satisfied with the consolation of her bosom, that you may drink deeply and be delighted with the abundance of her glory"* (Isaiah 66:7–11).

Two Signs

In Matthew 9, Mark 5, and Luke 8, we read of two incidents in the life of Jesus that took place on the same day and which can help us in our understanding of the two issues I have referred to – the cleansing (by atonement) of the land of Israel, and the raising up (by restoration) of the Jewish people to the promised land.

The First Sign – An Anonymous Lady

Jesus has been summoned by the Jewish ruler Jairus because his daughter, who is not named, is seriously ill. Jairus is desperate (quite understandably), he does not want his daughter to die, and so he asks Jesus to come to his home and heal his daughter.

Can a Nation be Born in a Day?

Walking along the road which leads to the home of Jairus, Jesus approaches a small rural community and as He does so, local people begin to emerge from their homes and workplaces. They want to see the Teacher who preaches the good news about the Kingdom of God. Also, many have heard that Jesus heals sick people and He has, according to some reports, even raised the dead.

As Jesus walks along the road, a small crowd quickly forms and follows Him. People continue to appear from all directions and the atmosphere soon becomes tense as the people jostle to get nearer to Jesus. For some, it seems, they, too, want Jesus to heal them.

Unknown by the crowd and to the disciples following Jesus and Jairus, a poor anonymous lady who is also desperate, is about to be thrown into the spotlight. This day, two miracles to meet two entirely different situations are about to take place.

At home and knowing nothing about what is taking place outside, this lady is unaware Jesus has been summoned by a religious leader and that He will soon be passing through her neighborhood.

Because of a long-standing physical ailment, a continuous discharge, which the *'Torah'* (her religion) has led to her being labeled as being *'unclean'* – indeed, her whole personal environment is considered as unclean – it's not easy for this lady to venture out to do shopping or to visit family or friends – not that she has many friends. Sadly, for twelve years, this Jewish lady has been treated as an outcast.

Having set the scene, imagine now a loyal and trusted friend knocking furiously on this lady's door. Perhaps trembling as to why someone is hammering on her door, nervously she lifts the latch and opens the door, just a little, to see who her visitor is. Her friend, who has always been kind and willing to help, informs her that Jesus is coming down the road and He is about to enter their village.

"Jesus, yes, it's Him, it's the teacher they call Jesus" she cries! *"Everyone is talking about Him; He has helped so many, many people, and He heals the sick. You must come – come quickly, before it's too late!"*

Taking her shawl from its nail beside the door, she closes the door and hastens down the road. From a distance she can see the crowd, like a swarm of ants moving as one, and somewhere in the middle of this throng of slowly moving humanity is the person this lady has so desperately wanted to meet, to speak to, to ask Him if He can help her. Maybe He could heal her, cleanse her? *"Will I be able to get near to Him? What will I say? What if He doesn't see me?"* So many questions race through her mind, while at the same time, concealed by her shawl, she is looking out in case someone might recognize her and point their finger, saying: *"She is unclean!"*

Can a Nation be Born in a Day?

Difficulty Number One

Because so many people are trying to approach Jesus, it seems impossible she will be able to get near Him. And because she is unclean, she has already decided not to speak to Him. If she is recognized, it would be difficult, because many in the crowd will know of her condition, which means by law all human contact is forbidden. This lady has known for twelve years, that because she is ritually unclean, that to touch another person will make them unclean (Haggai 2:13). Having been rejected by others has been so cruel, so hard; but to be rejected by Jesus? *"Oh, no!"*

Slowly our friend, who is now so anxious because she has waited twelve years for this opportunity to be healed, to be made clean, pushes her way to the centre of the crowd. Her plan, she has decided: *"I must draw near to Him, to Jesus."* (She has no *'Plan B'*).

Difficulty Number Two

Jesus is surrounded by a group of tough-looking men. She estimates there are about twelve of them and it seems as if they are acting as His personal bodyguard. To all appearances she now begins to doubt if it will be possible for her to draw near to Jesus. For twelve years she has suffered from an incurable condition, one which nobody has been able to help her with. It is a condition which has caused her much sorrow; and tears also. Why had this happened to her?

Struggling against the mass of the crowd, suddenly she sees her opportunity. Approaching Jesus from behind she has seen a small gap. *"If only I can get nearer to Him, I may be able to touch Him, or his clothing. There may never be another opportunity; it's my only chance!"* she says to herself. (But her conscience tells her to do so is forbidden; for contact with another person would make them unclean).

With a final and desperate attempt she reaches out (she has drawn near), and with her fingertips she manages to touch just the hem of His clothing. *"Yes, oh yes, I managed to touch Him!"* she says within herself. Although strictly forbidden, she knows that at last she has made contact with Jesus.

Disaster!

Jesus stops; everyone stops! Jesus turns and speaks: *"Who touched me?"* He asks. When those nearest to Him deny it, Peter (who has been impetuous before) says: *"Master, the multitudes throng and press You, and You say, 'Who touched Me?'"* (Luke 8:45).

Jesus, however, is aware that somebody in the crowd has touched Him, and that whoever it was, they must have had a reason for doing so. Jesus knows healing power has passed from Him to one individual, the person who deliberately touched Him. Why had they done so? Jesus is conscious that this was not an accident.

But should our friend remain silent and try to absence herself into the crowd, or should she identify herself and confess, at the risk of being ridiculed? Trembling, and with tears of gratitude flowing down her cheeks, she falls to her knees in front of Jesus. With Jesus standing in front of her and surrounded by such a vast throng of people, she confesses as to what she has just done. In the presence of Jesus, His twelve disciples, and so many witnesses, she pours out her story about why she had reached out to touch Him.

"Jesus, I had to draw near to You. I had to touch You, that's all I did, I simply touched You. Please, please, I want to be healed; I want to be cleansed."

Jesus' response was not to condemn her for what she had done, but with deep compassion and love for this lady of Israel (who represents Israel), He said to her: *"Daughter, your faith has made you well. Go in peace, and be healed of your affliction"* (Mark 5:34).

The first need (or sign) Jesus met on this historic day was to bring healing and cleansing to this lady. For twelve years she had suffered from a constant life-restricting and community rejecting discharge. When she first suspected something was wrong, she visited a local medical practitioner – to whom she had to pay a large fee – to seek help. The practitioner was unable to solve her problem and over a period of twelve years she visited numerous physicians, but had not experienced any improvement in her health.

Also during those twelve years, her finances had become seriously depleted, so that on the day she touched Jesus she had nothing left. Her savings, her human resources, they were all gone. But when she touched His clothing, she received both healing and cleansing. She knew, of course, it could only have happened because she had made up her mind what to do. Now healed and cleansed, she had no regrets.

Is there a reason why this lady had suffered from this particular ailment for twelve years? I suspect there is. Twelve in Hebrew and biblical terms is a perfect number and signifies: *'Perfection of Government'*. The number twelve is considered by Hebrew scholars as that which can scarcely be explained in words, but which the spiritual perception can appreciate as being: *'Organisation and Administration.'*

The following is a list of just a few examples of how the number twelve appears in the Bible.

1. Jacob was the father of twelve sons, and from their descendants were chosen the twelve tribes of Israel.

2. At Gilgal, Joshua set up twelve stones as a memorial to recall the children of Israel's entrance into the promised land.

3. Jesus chose twelve apostles – and the one who betrayed Him had to be replaced.

4. On the wall of the holy city Jerusalem will be twelve gates. Twelve angels will be at the gates and the names of the gates will be the names of the twelve tribes of Israel. The city will have twelve foundations, named after the twelve apostles of the Lamb. The twelve foundations will be twelve precious stones. The measurements of the city will be twelve thousand cubits its length, its breadth and its height. On the tree of life will be twelve crops of fruit in the twelve months of the year (Revelation 21 & 22).

When the number twelve appears in Scripture, it can include concealed meanings; thus encouraging us to delve deeper into the Bible's secrets. Having suffered shame for twelve years, this lady was considered to be unclean by her family, her neighbors and the religious fraternity. And, it is likely, she had only a few friends – so similar to Israel's position today. According to the book of Numbers, this lady should have been treated as an outcast. *"Command the children of Israel that they put out of the camp every leper and everyone who has a discharge"* (Numbers 5:2). Jesus, however, did not reject her, but with compassion He said to her – this lady who represented Israel – she was healed (cleansed) of her condition.

This account of a lady who had been branded as being unclean – and her possessions as being unclean – is an illustration of the polluted state of the land of Israel as described by God to Ezekiel. Remember, it was God who provided the illustration of the unclean woman (Ezekiel 36:17) and who likened her status as being akin to the condition of Israel.

It is not only in the Bible that such a description can be found. In 1947, the United Nations described the land that was then Palestine, as being neglected and despised, barren and forsaken. In 1947, the land soon to become Israel, was described by representatives from the nations as being a land that was unclean and unloved. It should come as no surprise that this land, which has now become loved and restored, is now looked upon by others with envy. Jealousy can cause immense difficulties and there can be no chance of peace with Israel unless this jealously is abandoned.

The Second Sign – Jairus' Daughter

Jairus' daughter was next and she was just twelve years of age. Born at the same time as when the lady had become unwell and unclean, is this just another of those Bible co-incidences, or was it because Jesus was aware on this particular day of what would eventually happen to the Jewish people in the nations to which they would be scattered? Was this a God-incident? I strongly believe that it was.

As recorded by Mark, Jairus, the little girl's father, said to Jesus: *"Come and lay Your hands on her, that she may be healed, <u>and she will live</u>"* (Mark 5:23).

Can a Nation be Born in a Day?

If you are familiar with these two miracles, have you ever wondered why we are not told the name of the lady, or the name of the twelve-year-old girl, but we do know the name of the father of the young girl – perhaps the least important person on this day? The name Jairus means: *'Ruler'*, and Jairus was the one who informed Jesus concerning his daughter: *"<u>And she will live</u>."* When God set Ezekiel down in the *'Valley of Dry Bones'*, He then informed Ezekiel: *"Surely, I will cause breath to enter into you <u>and you shall live</u>"* (Ezekiel 37:5).

At the time when Jairus first spoke to Jesus, he did so with conviction and with authority – he was living up to his name! What Jairus stated would happen, he believed by faith it would happen. It was with the same conviction and the same authority that God had earlier spoken to Ezekiel: *"Son of man, can these bones live?"* God knew that the bones could live, and when Ezekiel prophesied to the breath to inhabit the bones, it is then we read: *'And breath came into them, and they lived and <u>stood upon their feet</u>, an exceeding great army'* (Ezekiel 37:10).

Mark tells us that when Jesus took the little girl by the hand, *'Immediately the girl arose and walked* [she stood]*, for she was twelve years of age'* (Mark 5:42). Luke wrote: *'Then her spirit returned, and she arose* [she stood] *immediately'* (Luke 8:55). And in Ezekiel: *"I will put my Spirit in you, and you shall live, and I will place you in your own land. Then you shall know* *that I, the LORD, have spoken it and performed it, says the LORD"* (Ezekiel (37:14).

Two Illustrations – Two Signs

In the record of the life and work of Jesus, I believe we have confirmation that the two illustrations which God gave to Ezekiel would one day come to pass. First, the land would become healed and cleansed – as with the lady who was healed and cleansed of her discharge. Next, the people would be raised up, as if from the dead, to again live and stand in the land – illustrated by the twelve year old girl who, when Jesus took her by the hand, was raised from a state of death to be returned *on her feet* to those who had been involved in her birth. The reason? That she might live. What Jesus did for these two needy people, the lady and the young girl, strictly speaking was forbidden, for both were unclean. The lady had been suffering from a long-term discharge, and the twelve year old girl had died. Yet Jesus, on the same day, touched them both and restored them.

A few centuries earlier, Haggai was commanded by *'The LORD of Hosts'* to ask the priests a question concerning the Law. *"If one carries holy meat in the fold of his garment, and with the edge he touches bread or stew, wine or oil, or any food, will it become holy?" Then the priests answered and said, "No"* (Haggai 2:11–12). Under the Law of Moses, that which was considered holy could not by association make something which was unholy into something that was holy. However, with Jesus, this rule did not apply, because Jesus was, and is, infinitely holy, an attribute applying only to Him. What Jesus touched – or whoever touched Jesus – could become holy, or cleansed.

The involvement of Jesus in the cleansing of the unclean lady and the restoration of the young girl, is confirmation God has been involved in the atonement of the land of Israel and the people of Israel.

The circumstances of these two encounters Jesus had in the one day is so clear, so obvious, and illustrates that something which can scarcely be explained in words, but which the spiritual perception can at once appreciate, is recognized as: *'Divine Organisation and Administration'*. This is what the numeric twelve in its Hebrew meaning teaches us, and is why it is so relevant in these two miracles; both of which concern Israel the land and Israel its people.

The establishment of an independent Jewish state, known to Jewish people as: *'Eretz Israel'*, to which all Jewish people are welcome as they make Aliyah (*'Aliyah'* is the Hebrew word for the migration of Jewish people to Israel), is in fulfilment of the final words from the Song of Moses, which states that atonement for the land and atonement for the people will one day take place. It has now taken place (and continues to do so).

Israel Restored

Many of Israel's prophets, for example Isaiah and Jeremiah – but also Hosea (2:14–23 & 14:1–9), Joel (chapter 3), Amos (9:13–15), Obadiah (19–21), Micah (4:1–8), Zephaniah (3:14–20) and Zechariah (8:1–8 & 10:6–10) – wrote about this link that connects God's undertaking concerning the promised land and the Hebrew (Jewish) people. However, the prophet who was given two such detailed descriptions about God's relationship with this land and its people was the prophet Ezekiel.

For about 2,500 years, those who have had access to the book of Ezekiel have been able to read and take note of this ancient prophecy. From 70 CE (but especially from the late nineteenth century), many Jewish people and many Christians have prayed for its fulfilment.

God's intention, to cleanse the land and to bring about the restoration of the Jewish people to their ancient homeland, has taken place so that Gentiles might understand that what has happened to Israel has been an act of divine grace – His provision of atonement.

But also, the two miracles Jesus performed on the one day, and the establishment of the state of Israel on the one day (14th May 1948), are signs of God's authority in His pursuit of *'Perfection in Government'*.

This day, therefore – which I feel can be described as: *'A day of our Lord'* – the day when Jesus cleansed

Can a Nation be Born in a Day?

and healed an anonymous lady and then raised the daughter of Jairus from the dead (to show that Israel would also be restored), reminds me of the passage I quoted earlier, found in the last chapter of Isaiah.

'"Shall the earth be made to give birth in <u>one day</u>? Or shall a nation be born at once? For as Zion was in labor, she gave birth to her children. Shall I bring to the time of birth, and not cause delivery?" says the LORD. "Shall I who cause delivery shut up the womb?" says your God' (Isaiah 66:8–9).

Apart from creation, the birth of Israel on the one day (May 14th 1948) is almost certainly the clearest sign the world has that God exists, and that He should be honoured and respected by all.

This brings us to the final miracle Jesus performed; the raising of Lazarus from the dead. There is also a bonus – in the meaning of his name.

****

A THIRD SIGN – LAZARUS

Having concluded my thoughts about the lady Jesus healed, followed by the restoring to life of Jairus' daughter, I next felt an urge to consider a further day in the life of Jesus. I believe the Holy Spirit was saying: *"David, there is one more day in the life of Jesus which you need to understand."* Thus having received His prompting, I went to work and spent two hours pruning roses and tidying up the garden for one of my clients, the same gentleman who had asked me to cut down the three large trees. As I worked – I confess my thoughts were elsewhere! – the following episode held my undivided attention.

In John's Gospel we read the very detailed account of Jesus raising Lazarus from the dead. This miracle that Jesus performed portrays Him as being *'The Son of God'* – the giver of life. For readers who may not be aware for why there are four gospels in the New Testament, in his commentary on Matthew's Gospel, the author Charles Price explains.

1. Matthew portrays Jesus as *'King of Kings'*.

2. Mark as Jesus being *'The Suffering Servant'*.

3. Luke as Jesus being *'The Son of Man'*.

4. John as Jesus being *'The Son of God'*.

A Third Sign - Lazarus

Lazarus – A Friend of Jesus

Jesus is summoned by a messenger asking Him to go to Bethany because Lazarus, who is His friend, is unwell. However, although Lazarus is His friend, Jesus remains where He is and tells His disciples: *"This sickness is not unto death but for the glory of God, that the Son of God may be glorified through it"* (John 11:4). After waiting two days, Jesus said to His disciples He was now going to Bethany. His disciples advise Him that to do so would be reckless, because some of the religious Jews were planning to kill Him. Although Lazarus might die – and that would be a pity – in their opinion it was too dangerous for Jesus to go to Bethany. Jesus listened to what His disciples had to say and then explained to them why He was going to Bethany. It was not to make Lazarus better; rather it was because Lazarus was dead!

Let us now consider 2 Peter 3:8. Here Peter says to his readers: *'But, beloved, <u>do not forget this one thing</u>, that with the Lord one day is as a thousand years, and a thousand years as one day.'* Peter's words recall what the Psalmist wrote: *'For a thousand years in Your sight are like yesterday when it is past, and like a watch in the night'* (Psalm 90:4). May I suggest these two scriptures raises for us certain questions?

First, why did Jesus wait two days before divulging the news that Lazarus was now dead? Second, why only then was it the right time for Him to go Bethany to visit Lazarus at his grave? Why did Lazarus have to die? Was it not too late for Jesus to go to Bethany, knowing that His friend had died?

As I considered these questions, I felt it was important to know when it was that Jesus was born in relation to God's covenant with Abraham. Having arrived home from my work, it took only a few minutes to learn that Jesus was born 2,000 years after Abraham.

This raised an additional question. Was the 2,000 years from Abraham to Jesus, represented by the two days Jesus delayed His departure before going to visit Lazarus – His friend who was now dead? Within a few years (70 CE), Israel as a nation would also die, as Lazarus had died, even though their Messiah for whom Israel had been waiting had come.

When Jesus arrived in Bethany, He was greeted first by Martha. Martha said to Him: *"Lord, if you had been here, my brother would not have died"* (John 11:21). Jesus replied: *"Your brother will rise again"* (John 11:23). Jesus knew, before He arrived, that Lazarus was dead, and that it was now four days since he had been placed in the tomb (John 11:17).

Martha then went her way and called Mary, her sister, saying: *"The Teacher has come and is calling for you"* (John 11:28). *'Then when Mary came where Jesus was, and saw Him, she fell down at His feet, saying to Him, "Lord, if you had been here, my*

A Third Sign - Lazarus

brother would not have died"' (John 11:32). Note how Mary fell down at His feet. One day both Jews and Gentiles will fall down at His feet. Jesus then asked the two sisters where they had placed the body of their brother.

When Jesus drew near to the cave where they had laid Lazarus, He asked for the stone which had been used to seal the tomb, to be removed. Martha responded, saying that because her brother had been dead for four days, his body would have started to decay. Martha said to Jesus: *"Lord, by this time there is a stench, for he has been dead four days"* (John 11:39). Jesus, of course, would have known this, and He would also have known that according to the Torah (the Law given by God to Moses), that because Lazarus was now dead, he was considered as being unclean. Also, for anyone who touched Lazarus or his tomb, they, too, would become unclean. (Numbers 19:16–19).

According to this teaching in Numbers, anyone who had been in contact with a person who had died was to remain unclean for seven days. Meanwhile, a clean person would take a branch of hyssop, dip it in water, and on the third and the seventh days, sprinkle the one who was unclean in order to make him clean. He was also required to bathe and wash his clothes.

What an incredible picture this is of the Lord Jesus who, when He was suffering and taking our sin upon Himself, was approached by an unknown person who offered Him a drink of sour wine from a sponge fitted to a branch of hyssop (John 19:29). Although Jesus carried in His body the sins of the world when He died on the cross, He did not die as One who had sinned, or who was unclean, or who became unclean.

But let's return to Bethany and see what Jesus does next – after the stone had been removed. Standing a short distance from the tomb's entrance, Jesus cried out with a loud voice saying: *"Lazarus come forth!"* (John 11:43). And Lazarus came forth! Good news for Lazarus and his sisters, but what is the lesson in this miracle for the Jewish people and for Gentiles?

The Meaning of the Name Lazarus

Lazarus, I believe, is again representative of Israel – as the lady and the twelve year old girl also represents Israel. Concealed, however, because Lazarus appears in the New Testament, his name is given in the Greek rendering of what would have been his Hebrew name. This is unfortunate, because it hides the meaning of his name. In Hebrew, Lazarus' name was Eleazar, meaning: *'God has helped'*. In the Old Testament, Eleazar was one of the sons of Aaron who became a high priest. The name Eleazar reflects the calling and ministry of the high priest: *'One who represents God and whose calling is to help Israel'*.

In the New Testament, two men are named Lazarus; and the two are linked (in their function) to help the

A Third Sign - Lazarus

Jewish people and the Gentiles understand God's plans for His people and for the world.

The first Lazarus was a poor man who was laid at the gate of *'a certain rich man who was clothed in purple and fine linen and fared sumptuously every day'* (Luke 16:19). From this description, it appears Jesus may have been referring to Israel's privileged and wealthy high priest, who would have been clothed in purple and fine linen (see Exodus 39:1–8). If Jesus was implying this, then the poor man who was known as Lazarus – *'God has helped'* – was associated with the high priest through the meaning of his name.

The first Lazarus differs from the rich man, for after they had both died only Lazarus (of the parable) was carried by the angels to be with Abraham. When the rich man found himself in Hades and saw Abraham and Lazarus afar off, he pleaded with Abraham for him to send a messenger to his five brothers: *"If one goes to them from the dead, they will repent"* he said. Abraham, father of Israel, said to the rich man: *"If they do not hear Moses and the prophets, neither will they be persuaded though one rise from the dead"* (Luke 16:30–31). See also Luke 24:27.

A little later in Jesus' ministry – when Caiaphas was the high priest and Lazarus had been raised from the dead (John 11) – Caiaphas refused to accept the raising of Lazarus as a sign that Jesus was Israel's Messiah, but said it was necessary that both Jesus and

Lazarus should die (John 11:50 & 12:10). Caiaphas ignored what Moses and the prophets had written about Jesus, as Jesus explained in His teaching about the rich and their love of money (Luke 16:14–31).

In Jesus' teaching, the rich man not only regretted his own fate, but he was also concerned about his five brothers. In total there were six of them. In Hebrew thought, six is the number of man. Nearly 2,000 years later, six million Jews perished in the Holocaust. Are these two fiery events – the rich man's fate and the death of so many Jews – related? Possibly, but only God knows. What we do know is that in the early 1930s, a great evil came to power in Germany and as a result Jews (and Gentiles) suffered greatly.

I realise the explanation I have provided may appear complex, but what I have tried to do is to understand the connection between the two men who were named Lazarus – or *'Eleazar'* – and what their name in its Hebrew context means.

But are the two, one-and-the-same person?

I confess I do not consider myself to be an academic. It takes me a while to see things, but when I do, I try to understand if there is more to them than meets the eye. The conclusion I have come to only became clear after I had written the above. Therefore, to follow the sequence of how I first saw these things, I have decided to leave the prologue unchanged.

A Third Sign - Lazarus

Curious as to what Caiaphas' name means, I decided to investigate. From Wikipedia I learnt that his name means: *'To raise up'*. Was Caiaphas raised up – by who I do not know – to bring about the death Jesus? What we do know is that as a result of His death, because all have sinned, Jesus became our rescuer. Wikipedia also provided further details about Caiaphas. Josephus, the first-century Jewish historian and thought of as a reliable literary source of this period, recorded the dates of tenure of Israel's high priests from the year 6 CE to 63 CE. According to Josephus Caiaphas was the high priest in Jerusalem from 18 CE to 36 CE (i.e., Eighteen years, or three sixes – *'666 the perfection of imperfection of man'*).

Caiaphas' full name was: *'Joseph (son of) Caiaphas'*, but was known only as Caiaphas. Caiaphas married the daughter of Annas, who had been the high priest from 6 CE to 15 CE. According to Josephus, Annas was not only the father-in-law to Caiaphas, Annas also had five sons, and each of his sons became a high priest. Their names and years of tenure were:

1. Eleazar, son of Annas. 16–17 CE.

2. Jonathan, son of Annas. 36–37 & 44 CE.

3. Theophilus, son of Annas. 37–41 CE.

4. Matthias, son of Annas. 43 CE.

5. Ananus, son of Annas. 63 CE.

Lazarus and Caiaphas

Regarding Lazarus and Caiaphas, this is how I now see the role of these two men. In Luke we read of how Jesus portrays an after-life situation concerning a rich man and a poor man who had both died, but who were then separated in death. The poor man is named Lazarus. The rich man is not named.

The rich man, in his robes of purple and fine linen – was he Caiaphas the high priest? – pleaded with Abraham: *"I beg you therefore, father, that you send him* [Lazarus] *to my father's house* [his father-in-law Annas], *for I have five brothers* [his five brothers-in-law], *that he may testify to them, lest they also come to this place of torment"* (Luke 16:27–28).

When Jesus spoke to the Pharisees, I believe He knew precisely who He was referring to: Lazarus, Caiaphas, Annas, and the five sons of Annas. That the historical facts (available in the writings of Josephus) fit with the knowledge of Jesus which would later transpire, confirms Jesus was and is, Israel's Messiah.

It was not until I considered who the rich man was, that I came to see he was Caiaphas. Also, that his father (in-law) was Annas and his five brothers (in-law) were the sons of Annas as named by Josephus. Each of these eight men (including Lazarus) is a perfect casting in the parable Jesus presented to the Pharisees – and it included Abraham as Israel's father.

A Third Sign - Lazarus

Jesus Wept

When Jesus arrived at the tomb where Lazarus had been laid to rest, *'Jesus wept'* (John 11:35). Did Jesus weep for Lazarus who was about to emerge from the tomb alive and well? Possibly, but unlikely. Did Jesus weep for the two sisters of Lazarus because He shared in their sorrow? He may have. Or, did Jesus weep for Israel, knowing that many in Israel would soon die, and for the few who would survive, the majority of them would be taken into exile? If this was the case, His tears indicated He knew what was about to happen to His people. We now know that within just a few years Jerusalem was destroyed by the Romans and its inhabitants either killed, or driven into exile to become dispersed among the nations. It would then be nearly 2,000 years before their descendants would return to Eretz Israel, as it were from the grave. Was this the reason why Jesus wept? I believe it was.

When news of Lazarus being raised from the dead reached Jerusalem (just two miles from Bethany), Caiaphas, who was in league with his father-in-law Annas (John 18:13), said to the Pharisees: *"Do you consider that it is expedient for us that one man should die for the people, and not that the whole nation should perish?"* (see John 11:46–53).

At the time when Caiaphas prophesied the death of Jesus, he would not have known that his nation, for which his calling was to act as God's appointed representative, was about to perish, and that it would be nearly 2,000 years after the birth of the Man whom he proposed should die for the people – Israel's promised Messiah – that Israel would emerge, like Lazarus, from the grave. And also for those then living in Jerusalem, they would not have known that their descendants' return would not take place until 2,000 years later – and 4,000 years from when God made His covenant with Abraham.

A few days after Lazarus had been raised from the dead, when Jesus was being taken to Calvary to be crucified, Jesus spoke to a group of loyal women who were following Him, weeping and lamenting. He said to them: *"Daughters of Jerusalem, do not weep for Me, but weep for yourselves and for your children. For indeed the days are coming in which they will say, 'Blessed are the barren, the wombs that never bore, and breasts which never nursed!' Then they will begin to say to the mountains, 'Fall on us!' and to the hills, 'Cover us!' For if they do these things in the green wood, what will be done in the dry?"* (Luke 23:28–31).

His words to these women reflected His compassion for His people, for within a generation of Him dying, Jerusalem was destroyed and its people either killed or exiled. But also, His warning was in keeping with God's promise which I quoted earlier, from Isaiah 66:7–11, where Israel is likened to a woman giving birth in a day to a male child, and Zion giving birth to

A Third Sign - Lazarus

her children, and of them being consoled as they feed on the abundance of her glory in the latter days. Jesus also recalled the tree metaphor – *"For if they do these things in the green wood, what will be done in the dry?"* – as He warned these women that Israel, too, would become dry; as in the valley of dry bones as once seen by Ezekiel.

Is it possible that what Jesus said to these women who followed Him, when He informed them Jerusalem would one day be destroyed, that He had the miracle He had performed for Lazarus still fresh in His mind? Furthermore, the fall of Jerusalem would be followed by nearly 2,000 years of exile before Israel would rise from the dead, when survivors from the Holocaust would emerge in the way that history has recorded. History confirms that such an assumption is entirely possible. But why His tears – the shortest verse in the Bible? I believe Jesus' tears fulfilled what Jeremiah had been told by the LORD of Hosts.

*'Therefore thus says the LORD of hosts: "Behold, I will refine them and try them; for how shall I deal with the daughter of My people? Their tongue is an arrow shot out; it speaks deceit; one speaks peaceably to his neighbor with his mouth, but in his heart he lies in wait. Shall I not punish them for these things?" says the LORD. "Shall I not avenge Myself of such a nation as this? I will take up a **weeping and wailing** for the mountains, and for the dwelling places of the wilderness a lamentation, because they are*

burned up, so that no one can pass through; nor can men hear the voice of cattle. Both the birds of the heavens and the beasts have fled; they are gone. I will make Jerusalem a heap of ruins, a den of jackals. I will make the cities of Judah desolate, without an inhabitant" (Jeremiah 9:7–11). As God described the sinful depths to which Israel would one day descend – accompanied by His weeping and His wailing – so Jesus wept as His Father had wept. Yet they were not alone in their weeping for Israel.

*'Thus says the LORD of hosts: "Consider and call for **the mourning women**, that they may come; and send for skillful **wailing women**, that they may come. Let them make haste and take up a wailing for us, **that our eyes may run with tears, and our eyelids gush with water**. For a voice of wailing is heard from Zion; 'How we are plundered! We are greatly ashamed, because we have forsaken the land, because we have been cast out of our dwellings' "* (Jeremiah 9:17–19).

Do not these prophetic words speak (in part) of the tears of Jerusalem's women who wept for Jesus as they followed Him to His death, and who watched Him die for them and His accusers? Yet Jesus knew a more personal calamity for these women was about to descend upon Jerusalem; a calamity which God had instructed Jeremiah to record. Not long after Jesus was killed, Roman forces laid siege to Jerusalem, and following its fall, the city was destroyed and its citizens either killed or taken into exile.

A Third Sign - Lazarus

Jews and Gentiles

Gentile believers are indebted to the Jewish people because the Jewish Messiah has become the means whereby they can receive God's blessing. However, *'Has God cast away His people? Certainly not! God has not cast away His people whom He foreknew. I say then, have they stumbled that they should fall? Certainly not! But through their fall, to provoke them to jealousy, salvation has come to the Gentiles. Now if their fall is riches for the world, and their failure riches for the Gentiles, how much more their fullness! For if their being cast away is the reconciling of the world, what will their acceptance be but life from the dead?'* (Romans 11:1–2, 11–12 & 15).

Israel's rejection of their Messiah was followed by the Gentiles being given the opportunity to become God's people, through faith in Jesus – but Gentiles should not consider the Jews have been abandoned by God.

I can imagine the news that went around Jerusalem the day after Lazarus had been raised from the dead: *'Yesterday, Eleazar* [Lazarus], *who was taken ill four days ago and then died, has been raised from the dead! On the orders of Yeshua* [Jesus] *the Nazarene, the stone which had been used to seal the tomb where Eleazar was laid was removed. Following a command from Yeshua, Eleazar was seen to emerge from the tomb. After his grave-clothes had been removed, Eleazar was seen by many, walking unaided!'*

Israel Restored

I can also imagine the report in the Jerusalem Post on the morning of the 15th May, 1948, the day after Israel declared its Independence – just three years after the end of the Holocaust (three being the Hebrew number for resurrection). *'4,000 years after Abraham arrived in the promised land* [and 2,000 years after the birth of Jesus who had raised Lazarus from the dead] *Abraham's descendants* [his stars] *are back!'* Such a report could so easily have been supplemented by the words from Ezekiel 37:12–14.

"Therefore prophesy and say to them, 'Thus says the Lord God; "Behold, O My people, I will open your graves [reminding us of how the grave of Lazarus was opened] *and cause you to come up from your graves, and bring you into the land of Israel. Then you shall know that I am the LORD, when I have opened your graves, O My people, and brought you up from your graves. I will put My Spirit in you, and you shall live, and I will place you in your own land. Then you shall know that I, the LORD, have spoken and performed it, says the LORD.' "*

The fact Lazarus died and was buried, is a reminder that Israel would die, too, after their leaders rejected Jesus and the Romans (Gentiles) had crucified Him. About forty years later, when the Romans destroyed Jerusalem, its survivors were taken into exile. Not until 1948 would the Jews be restored to their land, and by a United Nations resolution, however, it would not be until nineteen years later, 1967, that the words

A Third Sign - Lazarus

of Jesus: *"And Jerusalem will be trampled by the Gentiles until the times of the Gentiles are fulfilled* (Luke 21:24) would come to pass.

Significantly, approximately 2,000 years elapsed from God's calling of Abraham to the time of Jesus' birth; and 2,000 years has elapsed from His birth to Israel's restoration. i.e., 4,000 years (four days) in total.

Return Backsliding Israel

Just three years after the war in Europe ended, during which a thick darkness like that of a tomb descended upon the Jewish people, Israel as a nation rose from the dead. Those who were already its inhabitants formed the stump which had remained in the ground during those turbulent years; whereas some of the new inhabitants were among those who had survived the Holocaust and who came to Israel after the war. When Israel appeared again in the world's arena, the time was right for it to respond to God's earlier call through His servant Jeremiah of the need to repent of its backsliding.

'The LORD said also to me in the days of Josiah the king: "Have you seen what <u>backsliding</u> Israel has done?" [Jeremiah 3:6]. *"Then I saw that for all the causes for which <u>backsliding</u> Israel had committed adultery"* [Jeremiah 3:8]. *'Then the LORD said to me, "<u>Backsliding</u> Israel has shown herself more righteous than treacherous Judah. Go proclaim these words*

toward the north, and say: 'Return, <u>backsliding</u> Israel', says the LORD; 'I will not cause my anger to fall on you. For I am merciful,' says the LORD; I will not remain angry forever" [Jeremiah 3:11 & 12]. *"Return, O <u>backsliding</u> children", says the LORD; for I am married to you"* [Jeremiah 3:14]. *"Return, you <u>backsliding</u> children, and I will heal your <u>backslidings</u>"* [Jeremiah 3:22].

The reason why I have emphasized these references in Jeremiah to Israel's backsliding, is because when we see repetition in the Bible, there is usually a reason. Here, I suspect, it is especially so.

For Christians, John chapter three has always been a much-loved chapter. For Israel, Jeremiah chapter three is also very important. *'Will you not from this time cry to Me, "My Father, you are the guide of my youth?"* (Jeremiah 3:4). God's plea is for the children of Israel to return from their backsliding – which, ideally, will lead to them responding as follows: *"For we have sinned against the LORD our God, we and our fathers, from our youth even to this day, and have not obeyed the voice of the LORD our God"* (Jeremiah 3:25).

Israel and Jesus

In 1948 when Jewish people were restored to their land, only a few believed in Jesus as God's Son, their long-awaited Messiah. Since 1948, many have come

A Third Sign - Lazarus

to faith, so that today there are a considerable number of Messianic believers in Israel. Some have joined large congregations, while others, not wanting to copy the Gentile's system of churches, meet in homes.

Religious Fervour

In June 1967, Israel was forced into a war with its neighbours because they were intent on Israel's destruction. The war was not of Israel's choosing, but Israel was victorious. After the war, Israel Weinberg, Deputy Director General of the Ministry for Religious Affairs, wrote, *'Because of the war, there is not one individual in this country who does not believe in God'*. On August 20th 1967, the Sunday Times reported that following the 1967 war: *'Victorious Israel was being swept by religious fervour and intense faith in divine guidance.'*

Since 1967 there has been a growing awareness of God in Israel's mixed community – partly based on the evidence of the Jewish people being restored to their land. God, however, was never at fault. 2,000 years ago, Jesus informed Israel that He was: *"The way, the truth and the life"* and that He had come to cleanse and redeem Israel in a covenant of God's goodness and His mercy. At the time, Israel's leaders, including Caiaphas, refused to listen to or to take heed of the signs. Caiaphas and his friends rejected (or ignored) the evidence of the resurrection of Lazarus; once the stone had been removed from his tomb. They also rejected the words from one of their most popular Psalms: *'The stone which the builders rejected has become the chief cornerstone. This was the LORD's doing; it is marvelous in our eyes. This is the day which the LORD has made; we will rejoice and be glad in it'* (Psalm 118:22–24).

The tomb of Jesus (as with the tomb of Lazarus) was covered by a stone, which Caiaphas was determined should remain in place by sealing it and mounting a guard at the tomb's entrance. His efforts, however, were thwarted; this time it was an angel who moved the stone! (Matthew 27:62–66 and Matthew 28:2).

Temporary Blindness

I am aware of a few who believe God has abandoned the Jews in favour of the Gentiles; but this was never the case, nor was it ever intended. It is now four thousand years (*four days*) since God covenanted with Abraham, and today, two thousand years (*two days)* after Jesus was born, God is gradually removing the blindness from the eyes of the Jewish people. This is so similar to what Jesus did for Lazarus when He raised him from the dead. *'And he who had died came out bound hand and foot with grave-clothes, and his face was wrapped with a cloth. Jesus said to them, "Loose him, and let him go"'* (John 11:44). After the four days, when the cloth was removed from the face of Lazarus, instead of the blindness caused by death and the darkness of tomb, Lazarus could see.

Paul when writing to Christians in Rome – from the same chapter I quoted earlier – wrote: *'For I do not desire, brethren, that you should be ignorant of this mystery, lest you should be wise in your own opinion, <u>that blindness in part has happened to Israel</u> until the fullness of the Gentiles has come in'* (Romans 11:25).

If God is for Israel and the Jewish people – which I believe He is – their eyes will continue to be opened to see that Jesus is their one and only living hope; He who died on the cross for both Jew and Gentile and who has enabled Israel to rise from the dead and see.

What Jesus did for Lazarus is the same as in Ezekiel's vision of the Valley of Dry Bones (Ezekiel 37:10–14) and that of the Jewish people. A new way of living after being made clean is what the work of atonement is for. Atonement is a gift from God.

Joseph – a Hebrew Servant

In this chapter, I have suggested the two men called Lazarus are in fact one-and-the-same. In a similar way Pharaoh's two dreams which Joseph interpreted were also one-and-the-same (Genesis 41:25). But as Joseph said to Pharaoh, their interpretation was not in him (Genesis 41:16). Joseph, a Hebrew, was only able to provide Pharaoh with the interpretation of his two dreams because God was with him and had shown Pharaoh what He was about to do.

****

LESSONS FROM HISTORY

Before finally delving into why the Jewish people have been returned to the promised land, I would like to point out that there exists in history a lesson which most non-Jewish people have still not grasped.

From my own perception, World War Two began on the 9th November, 1938, the night Hitler declared war on Germany's Jews – *'Kristallnacht'*. However, what has often been overlooked is a conference which took place four months earlier, in July 1938.

Following Hitler's rise to power, one of his first acts was to turn against Germany's 900,000 Jews – who soon became aware of the danger they were in. Their problem, however, there were very few places where they could escape to. Britain still opposed large scale emigration to their *'League of Nations'* protectorate in Palestine, and most other countries were reluctant to take in a large number of Germany's Jews.

As the crisis deepened, an international conference was hastily arranged and thirty two countries sent delegates to discuss quotas of German Jews they were prepared to accept. The conference (6–15 July 1938), was held in the French city of Evian, on the French side of Lake Geneva. Hitler, it had been reported, was willing for Germany's Jews to leave Germany if other countries would accept them. Most were not, although Costa Rica and the Dominion Republic did increase their quota of Jews they were willing to take in.

The fact most countries were not prepared to accept increased Jewish migration, resulted in the German delegation returning to Germany and (it is said) saying to Hitler: *"You can do what you like with the Jews; nobody wants them."* For Hitler, it was a huge boost in his campaign to rid Germany of its Jews. Four months later, *'Kristallnacht'*, the burning of hundreds (some say a thousand) of synagogues took place. During the pogrom, many Jewish businesses and homes were ransacked and many Jews died.

Regarding this largely forgotten lesson, what was it? The lesson can be found in the name of the city where the conference was held. By taking the letters *'Evian'* and reversing them, we get the word *'naïve'* – which means: *'Gullible'*. At Evian in July 1938, naivety was where the European seed of war began to germinate.

In Golda Meir's autobiography, *'My Life'* (1975), Meir, who attended the conference in an unofficial capacity, reported to press delegates: *"There is only one thing I hope to see before I die, and that is that my people should not need expressions of sympathy anymore."* Chaim Weizmann, the Jew who rescued Britain during the crisis of the First World War, told the Manchester Guardian newspaper: *"The world seemed to be divided into two parts – those places where the Jews could not live, and those where they could not enter."* Another observer, Walter Mondale, wrote: *'At stake at Evian were human lives and the decency and self respect of the civilized world.'*

When it came to rescuing Germany's Jews, the world failed them miserably – so there were consequences.

The Consequences of Evian

I can remember only one occasion when I broke down in a public place to shed tears copiously. It happened on the 7th June 2007 at the Yad Vashem Holocaust museum in Jerusalem. The name Yad Vashem is taken from Isaiah (56:5) and translates: *'To them will I give in My house and within My walls, a place and a name that shall not be cut off.'* Fortunately, Janet my wife, my friend from when we were at school together in the late 1950s was nearby and duly responded to my need for comfort.

The reason for my distress came as I was watching a film being played on a video monitor which showed the liberation by British forces of the Bergen Belsen concentration camp. Since the 1970s, I have watched a number of films about the Holocaust, but never before have I known such sadness. I recall going to see *'Schindler's List'* with our friend Dot. Dot sat to my left and Janet was on my right. At one point in the film (a very difficult scene), it was just too much for Dot and she clung to my arm in tears.

Whilst I understood Dot's need to shed tears, my own eyes remained dry. My eyes have usually remained dry, even when watching films such as *'The Pianist'* and documentary films about the Holocaust. But at Yad Vashem it was my turn to weep. The scene which reduced me to tears was of a large bulldozer pushing scores of emaciated bodies into a deep trench.

Bulldozers are normally used to push stones into holes; but to see people, not dummies, with broken limbs and emaciated bodies being pushed along by a powerful bulldozer was just too much – tears tumbled down my cheeks and into my hands. Traumatized by what I had seen, I turned from the monitor; it was too horrific to watch any more. Death is something we must all face, but it is a tragedy that so many lives were cut-off in such a short period of time and in such a brutal way because of racial and religious hatred.

The evil of the Holocaust resulted in immense pain for those who became its victims; for those who were killed, but also the survivors. What is baffling is that so many plain and ordinary people were willing to become executioners and to murder (seemingly without conscience) men, women and little children.

Because of the suffering inflicted on Europe's Jews, I feel it appropriate to recall two incidents.

In September 1941, German troops entered the city of Kiev. In a well-documented account of mass murder which was carried out over a two day period (29–30 September, 1941), 33,771 Jews were slaughtered. This mass killing of Jewish people was the largest single atrocity carried out by the Nazi regime during its campaign in the Soviet Union. Still remembered as *'The Babi-Yar Massacre'*, the decision to kill the Jews in Kiev was taken by Major General Kurt Eberhard. The victims were forced into a ravine – *'Babi-Yar'* – and shot. During the killings, the bodies became piled on top of each other in layers before being covered with soil. Of Kiev's tens of thousands of Jews, we now know very few of them survived the war.

At the other end of the scale (numbers), the entire Jewish community in Tromso, Norway, just eighteen souls, the youngest of which was only two-and-a-half years old, were rounded up by the Gestapo and sent to Auschwitz. Not one of them survived.

The history of the Holocaust in Europe has been well documented, because as has been said many times: *"It must never happen again."* What is worth noting is Israel's re-birth took place three years and one week after the Second World War in Europe ended. During the six years and six months of the war, as Gentile nations became rooted to the abyss they had created; simultaneously, the darkness was being added to as Abraham's stars were being extinguished. Three years later when it was all over (1948), Israel was restored. It was the right time for those who had survived the nightmare of the Holocaust to rise – as Lazarus had risen alive from his tomb. In the Hebrew idiom, three is the number for resurrection.

Was it known that Israel would be born in a day? The answer is *'Yes'* (Isaiah 66:8). Seven years later (1955) I purchased a second-hand book at a church jumble sale featuring two photographs of the Holocaust that were to make such a long-lasting impression on me. Was there ever a cleansing and a resurrection such as this? Indeed so; first the lady who Jesus healed, then the daughter of Jairus who had died – and both miracles took place on the same day. But let us not forget Lazarus' resurrection. Here we have three signs of the granting of atonement for Israel, the land and its people, as God had earlier indicated to Moses.

What can be achieved by war?

In reflecting on the twentieth century's two major conflicts – the first of which a number of historians have said achieved little, the second which Churchill said was unnecessary and could so easily have been stopped – observers might ask themselves: *"Have any lessons been learnt from these two wars?"* Apparently not, not if we consider history's experience.

Egypt

The first recorded case of anti-Semitism can be found in Exodus chapter one. Because the children of Israel had become firmly established in Egypt, and their loyalty in time of war was seen by Pharaoh as being unknown, Pharaoh decided to limit what he perceived as a threat to his people. Thus the children of Israel were forced by the Egyptians to become slaves and to build for them their cities. Despite this hostility, they continued to increase in numbers; and so Pharaoh ordered that when the Hebrew mothers were about to give birth, their midwives were to kill the baby boys. However, the midwives feared God more than they feared Pharaoh, so did everything they could to avoid killing the young boys.

As a baby, Moses was one of those who should have been killed, but he was saved by being placed in a waterproof basket and placed in the Nile. Pharaoh's daughter then rescued Moses and adopted him as her son. When Moses was forty years of age, he saw an Egyptian mistreating a Hebrew slave, and because he killed the Egyptian, he was forced to flee from Egypt. Forty years later, when Moses returned to Egypt, he was instrumental in persuading Pharaoh to let the children of Israel go free; but only after Pharaoh had paid a very high price for his stubbornness. Because Pharaoh repeatedly refused Moses' request for the children of Israel to go into the wilderness to worship God, his first-born son and those of the Egyptians died. His stubbornness resulted in Egypt's loss.

Turkey

In June 1896, Theodor Herzl visited Constantinople and tried to negotiate with Sultan Abdul Hamid II in order to establish a Jewish homeland in Palestine. The Sultan refused to co-operate. Within a within a few years (1917), Britain seized Palestine from Turkey. Because of his stubbornness, it was Turkey's loss.

Germany

Since September 11th 2001, the euphemism *'9/11'* has been indelibly associated with militant Islam – what (suicide) extremists are prepared to do to promote their dogma. However, the *'9/11'* of 2001, when three thousand people were killed in suicide attacks on Washington D.C. and the World Trade Center in New York, was not the first time a major terrorist incident has become associated with these two numbers. Sixty-three years earlier, Jewish people were the target of a hate-filled pogrom on *'9/11'*.

In a night of terror known as *'The Night of Broken Glass'*, Jewish homes, businesses and synagogues – places of worship – were destroyed during the night of 9th November, 1938. It was the night when Hitler began his campaign to wage war on Germany's Jews. Hitler personally sanctioned the attacks, during which many Hebrew scriptures were taken from hundreds of synagogues and set alight in huge bonfires.

Next to be consumed by the flames (burning) were the synagogues. Finally, a few years later, over a period of years, it was the turn of Jewish men women and children to be consumed in the Nazi's crematoria.

In Frederick Taylor's book *'Dresden'*, in which he describes the events leading up to *'Kristallnacht'*, Taylor describes the burning of Dresden's much-loved Gottfried Semper's Synagogue, situated beside the river Elbe. Taylor also refers to a Dresden street character named Franz Hackel. Hackle's friend, the artist Otto Griebel, joined Hackel on the banks of the Elbe as they watched the synagogue destroyed. As they did so, Hackel turned to his friend and said: *"This fire will return! It will make a long curve and then come back to us!"* Just over six years later, on the night of 13/14 February, 1945, only a matter of a few weeks before the war in Europe ended, Dresden was bombed and destroyed in a huge fire as Hackel had predicted. *'Kristallnacht'* (*9/11*), the burning of books and synagogues, had been a crime against God.

Hitler's dream was to provide the German people with more living space – *'Lebensraum'* – and for the establishment of a thousand-year Reich. But Hitler was misguided and his dream ended in a bunker in Berlin when he committed suicide. Hitler, a coward, was unwilling to face his people (or his adversaries) and he brought death and destruction to Germany. His ruthlessness and his stubbornness led to Germany's loss.

Britain

During the 1920s and to 1947, Britain, using physical force, restricted the passage of Jews into Palestine, despite having promised in 1917 to do so. On the 3rd September, 1939, Britain declared war on Germany.

After a long drawn-out war Britain achieved success, but still continued to frustrate Jewish settlement in Palestine. Soon after the war, Britain witnessed the rapid dismantling of its world-wide Empire. Britain's stubbornness was followed by her loss of Empire.

Israel and its Neighbours

It's time to bring things up-to-date. For Israel (and this applies to other Middle East countries), it seems there is no solution to the question regarding who is to live where – and so the arguments and the various conflicts continue. But could it have been different; was peace between Israel and her neighbours ever achievable? The answer is a definite: *'Yes, there could have been peace'*, and in the year 2000 a lasting peace settlement was certainly possible.

In 1999, Ehud Barak was elected as Prime Minister of Israel. During the following year, 2000, Barak and his government tried their utmost to come to a settlement with the Palestinians at the Camp David Conference. Yasser Arafat, the leader of the Palestinians, although promised 98% of the territory he was demanding, turned down Israel's undertaking to make concessions for peace. By walking away from his greatest chance to bring peace and prosperity to his people, Arafat ended the Oslo peace process.

Shortly after the breakdown in negotiations, Arafat declared war on Israel, and so began the Al-Aqsa Intifada. In his book, *'Fast Facts on the Middle East Conflict'* (2003), Randall Price quotes the defence analyst Ze'ev Schiff: *'Among the Arabs there is an increasing feeling that they have hit on the formula for bringing Israel to its knees.'* Schiff explained: *'Ongoing, low-level war that combines massive terrorism, guerrilla warfare and the international media ... this strategy will expose Israel's Achilles' heel, and extreme sensitivity to loss of life and the kidnapping* [and murder] *of its soldiers.'* More than a decade later, similar methods are still being used by militants who are diametrically opposed to Israel's existence. As a result of hatred and stubbornness, it has been the Palestinians' loss.

No weapon formed against you (Israel) shall prosper

The danger of not heeding the sufferings of others – which applies to all extremist groups – is that they risk making the same mistakes that others have made in opposing Israel. The Bible's message about going to war with Israel is very clear: *"No weapon formed against you shall prosper"* (Isaiah 54:17); yet as history has shown, it has too often been ignored.

Because of the killing of Jewish people and the theft and/or destruction of their property during the six years and six months of the Second World War, for those who survived, they knew the only place where they could find safety from their enemies was for them to flee to Zion, a tiny area of land located at the eastern end of the Mediterranean Sea and which had been allocated to them by God.

Jerusalem – Who does it belong to?

Many years ago, God made known to His servant Zechariah, His future plans for Jerusalem. When Zechariah *'raised his eyes'*, he saw a man going out to measure Jerusalem. Then an angel spoke to the prophet and gave him a message from the Lord. Because the dialogue is so riveting – for it concerns Jerusalem – I have decided to quote it in full.

'Then I raised my eyes and looked, and behold, a man with a measuring line in his hand. So I said, "Where are you going?" And he said to me, "To measure Jerusalem, to see what is its width and what is its length." And there was the angel who talked with me, going out; and another angel was coming out to meet him, who said to him, "Run, speak to this young man, saying: 'Jerusalem shall be inhabited as towns without walls, because of the multitude of men and livestock in it.' 'For I,' says the LORD, 'will be a wall of fire around her, and I will glory in her midst'" (Zechariah 2:1–5).

The Lord continues: *"Up, up! Flee from the land of the north,"* says the LORD; *"for I have spread you abroad like the four winds of heaven,"* says the

*LORD. "Up, Zion! Escape, you who dwell with the daughter of Babylon." For thus says the LORD of hosts: "He sent Me after glory, to the nations which plunder you; **for he who touches you touches the apple** [the pupil] **of His eye**. For surely I will shake My hand against them, and they shall become spoil for their servants. Then you will know that the LORD of hosts has sent Me. Sing and rejoice, O daughter of Zion! For behold, I am coming and I will dwell in your midst," says the LORD. "Many nations shall be joined to the LORD in that day, and they shall become My people. And I will dwell in your midst. Then you will know that the LORD of hosts has sent Me to you. And the LORD will take possession of Judah as His inheritance in the Holy Land, and will again choose Jerusalem* [referring to His promise to king David]. *Be silent, all flesh, before the LORD, for He is aroused from His holy habitation!"* (Zechariah 2:6–13).

Isaac and Lazarus

God's choice of Jerusalem (and His provision for its atonement), dates from when Abraham offered up his only begotten son, *'Concluding that God was able to raise him up, even from the dead, from which he also received him in a figurative sense'* (Hebrews 11:17–18). Because Abraham did not hesitate to withhold his son (Genesis 22:16), the Angel of the Lord intervened and told Abraham not to sacrifice Isaac. The timing was three days from when Abraham had set out on his journey to the place where he was to offer up Isaac – Mount Moriah. We know of it today as the Temple Mount in Jerusalem.

'Then Abraham lifted his eyes and looked, and there behind him was a ram caught in a thicket by its horns. So Abraham went and took the ram, and offered it up for a burnt offering instead of his son. And Abraham called the name of the place, The-LORD-Will-Provide; as it is said to this day, "In the Mount of the LORD it shall be provided."' (Genesis 22:13–14). This *'Mount of the LORD'* and Jerusalem as being God's city was confirmed by God with an oath with His servant David: *"Yet I have chosen Jerusalem, that My name may be there"* (2 Chronicles 6:6).

Prior to when Abraham took a ram and offered it as a substitute for his son, Abraham had bound Isaac and laid him on the altar upon the wood (Genesis 22:9). With God's provision of a ram, Abraham then loosed his son Isaac from his bonds to allow him to go free. 2,000 years later when Lazarus emerged from a tomb in Bethany with his face wrapped in a cloth, Jesus said to those who had rolled the stone away: *"Loose him, and let him go* [free]*"* (John 11:44).

Lazarus, who would have been in darkness for four days, would have needed time to adjust his eyes to the light, and in all likelihood the first person he would have seen would be Jesus, who within a few days time would also die. It was He of whom John the Baptist had said: *"Behold! The Lamb of God who takes away the sin of the world!"* (John 1:29). Later, at Calvary, Lazarus may well have seen Jesus with a crown of thorns on His head, and if so, he may have recalled the ram Abraham had sacrificed in the stead of his son Isaac – who became the father of Jacob and whose name God changed to Israel (Genesis 32:28). Isaac was indeed a forerunner of both Lazarus and Jesus. Abraham's eyes – *'He looked'* – became focused as he saw God's provision of a ram. Lazarus' eyes, too, would have become focused as he saw God's provision of *'The Lamb of God'*, the Lord Jesus.

Today we are approximately 2,000 years from when Jesus was born for Him to be offered up as a Passover sacrifice for the sins of the world – then raised from the dead like the figurative raising of Abraham's son Isaac. Surely, now is the perfect time for Israel's eyes to be opened to see Jesus, their Messiah and Saviour, because they, too, as God's people have been raised from the dead.

When Jesus died, the veil of the temple was torn in two. It happened, as the writer of Hebrews says: *'Let us therefore come boldly to the throne of grace, that we may obtain mercy and find grace to help in time of need'* (Hebrews 4:16). Because Jesus died, today is a good time for this generation to seek God.

What is so evident in God's illustration of the unclean woman (Ezekiel 36:17) and the Valley of Dry Bones

(Ezekiel 37), is that the cleansing and healing process has been taking place precisely as Jesus demonstrated. As we have seen, it has always been God's intention that His people – those who have been persecuted by the Gentile nations (especially in Russia and Europe during centuries of anti-Semitism) – be restored to their rightful inheritance as shown in the miracles Jesus performed in the cleansing of the lady and the raising up of the daughter of Jairus. But also, the resurrection of Lazarus had an important part to play in illustrating Israel's eventual restoration.

Despite biased and politically motivated action being taken against Israel (e.g., boycotts of Israeli goods), one thing needs to be remembered about Israel's God – God is Holy. Man does not have the intrinsic nature of holiness which God possesses. Isaiah was aware of this, and so he wrote: *'But we are all like an unclean thing, and all our righteousnesses are like filthy rags'* (Isaiah 64:6).

The rags referred to here (as the Complete Jewish Bible renders this verse), are menstruation rags, and would have been a daily requirement for the lady who Jesus cleansed and healed. The fact for twelve years this lady had suffered from this unpleasant condition is a reminder of what Isaiah wrote about God's loving-concern for His people. If ever there was a God-inspired warning to Israel about their rebellion and their sin – still a present-day offence – surely it is expressed in the first six chapters of Isaiah? It is from the first chapter of Isaiah that we see how God urges Israel to: *"Wash yourselves, make yourselves clean; put away the evil of your doings from before my eyes"* (Isaiah 1:16). It is a well-known and often quoted saying that cleanliness and godliness go together.

Sadly, God would have known there would only be a partial response to His pleading, and that eventually the abject cruelty of the Holocaust would consume many of His people. But not everyone – one tenth would remain safe in God's hands, and because they were safe, they were not for consuming.

The Gold Train

For many today, although they may be familiar with some of the things which happened to the Jews during the Holocaust (they may have read or seen films about the Holocaust), such familiarity can never bring them to an understanding of the extent of their sufferings, no matter how hard they try. God, however, provided numerous warnings about what would happen if Israel continued to ignore His laws and the messages He gave to His servants. In the third chapter of Isaiah, God's servant describes the plunder of God's people's possessions, what they regarded as being their most precious belongings.

'In that day the Lord will take away the finery: The jingling anklets, the scarves, and the crescents; the pendants, the bracelets, and the veils; the

headdresses, the leg ornaments, and the headbands; the perfume boxes, the charms, and the rings; the nose jewels, the festal apparel, and the mantles; and the mirrors; the fine linen, the turbans, and the robes' (Isaiah 3:18–23).

In this passage, the attention to detail is striking. In June 2003, the writer Ronald Zweig published his book *'The Gold Train'*, in which he describes how from hundreds of thousands of Hungarian Jews, gold, silver, jewelry and clothing was loaded onto a train and transported to one of the Nazis' secret hideouts. Zweig provides a fascinating insight into the closing stages of fascist Europe and of the post-war period as the world attempted to come to terms with the murder of 400,000 Hungarian Jews. More recently, my wife and I went to see the film, *'The Monuments Men'*. This film is based on the true story of how a team of experts searched for where gold and other valuables which had been stolen by the Nazis (mainly from Jews) had been hidden, and to return the items to their rightful owners. By the end of the war, however, most of the dispossessed had been killed, and so there were few opportunities to act justly and return the stolen items to their rightful owners.

This word of the Lord in Isaiah three continues: *'And so it shall be: Instead of a sweet smell there will be a stench* [the stench of the death camps. This reminded me of what Martha said to Jesus regarding her brother Lazarus: *"Lord, by this time there is stench, for he has been dead for four days"]. Instead of a sash, a rope* [for hanging]. *Instead of well-set hair, baldness* [head shaving]. *Instead of a rich robe, a girding of sackcloth* [prison clothing]. *And branding instead of beauty* [the tattooing of the arms of Jews with a number]. *Your men shall fall by the sword, and your mighty <u>in the war</u>. Her gates shall lament and mourn, and she being desolate <u>shall sit on the ground</u>'* (Isaiah 3:24–26). Just how many images (photographs and films) are there, of Jews being forced to sit on the ground as they waited for the trains to take them to the death camps? The age of photography has been a timely way of reminding us of this ancient prophecy.

The Word of God (including the words of Jesus) is both historical and authoritative when it comes to describing the terms and conditions which apply to those who are meant to possess the promised land. The reason for this is quite simple; for in the final analysis it is a question of who owns the land – is it God or man? For those who profess to know and want to serve God, there is a responsibility to respect God's plans for Israel – the land and its people. For those who do not know or understand God, they are likely to be misinformed and therefore misled.

For our lady, she who followed Jesus, in the morning when she awoke, there was no longer any discharge, no more blood, no unclean rags to be destroyed by burning. Surely, she must have been overjoyed and would have told all she knew it had been Jesus who had cleansed and restored her? The reason for her joy was that she had reached out in faith to the One she had heard about, the God-man called Jesus. For her, as with the imagery of what Isaiah wrote concerning God's promise to Israel, His words are as recorded (again) in the first chapter of Isaiah.

'"Come now, and let us reason together," Says the LORD, "Though your sins are like scarlet, they shall be as white as snow; though they are red like crimson [blood]*, they shall be as wool. If you are willing and obedient, you shall eat of the good of the land; but if you refuse and rebel, you shall be devoured by the sword"; for the mouth of the LORD has spoken'* (Isaiah 1:18–20).

The first part of this appeal in Isaiah recalls the lady who Jesus cleansed from her continuous discharge (bleeding). It also describes the efficacious love of Jesus – *'To Him who loved us and washed us from our sins <u>in His own blood</u>'* – when He died for us (Revelation 1:5). But then in the second part of this appeal, the blessings of God for the obedient, and the warnings of God for the disobedient, are reminiscent of what is written in Deuteronomy (chapter 28).

The Reliability of The Bible

What hope, therefore, can Jewish people and Gentiles look forward to? Inseparably, hope is linked to faith, for faith enables us to trust in Jesus and His mission to bring us into union with His Father and with Himself through the work of the Holy Spirit. This is why, as Jesus said to Nicodemus: *'You must be born again'* (John 3:7). But also, as Paul wrote to the believers in Rome: *'For I am not ashamed of the gospel of Christ, for it is the power of God to salvation for everyone who believes, for the Jew first and also for the Greek [Gentile]'* (Romans 1:16).

When communicating God's Word to Israel, Isaiah recorded: *"For as the rain comes down, and the snow from heaven, and do not return there, but water the earth, and make it bring forth and bud, that it may give seed to the sower and bread to the eater, so shall My word be that goes forth from My mouth; it shall not return to Me void, but it shall accomplish what I please, and it shall prosper in the thing for which I sent it"* (Isaiah 55:10–11).

What first happened to Isaac (figuratively), Lazarus, and then Jesus, and in a similar way has happened to the Jewish people – their death and resurrection – is proof that God is faithful in keeping His Word – *"It shall not return to Me void"* – for God can be trusted by all who believe in Him and in His Son, the Lord Jesus, if they are willing to respect Him, trust Him, and keep His Word.

****

Lessons From History

The entrance to Dresden's new synagogue. Sealed in a panel above the entrance is a *'Star of David'*, the only item that was recovered from the previous synagogue when it was destroyed by fire on 9/11/1938 – *'Kristallnacht'*.

The clouds which are reflected in the glass above the doors, reminded me when I visited the new synagogue, of the clouds of darkness which descended on Europe on this fateful night. This symbol of Jewish life was removed from the ruins of the original synagogue by a fireman, who then hid it in his loft until the end of the war.

ISRAEL'S DECLARATION OF INDEPENDENCE

To complete the material contained in this book, I considered it appropriate to include the wording of Israel's Declaration of Independence (1948). Whilst I understand some of the difficulties the restoration of Israel has caused, nevertheless, it has been a modern day miracle, such as that experienced by the lady with the discharge, Jairus' daughter who died, and Lazarus. I also believe that if non-Jews who live in the Middle East – including those who are known as Palestinians – wanted to experience peace with Israel, then the two communities could live together in harmony. There are, unfortunately, those who have no intention of ever making peace with Israel.

On the 14th May, 1948, David Ben-Gurion, Israel's primary founder and the first Prime Minister of Israel, announced the terms of Israel's Declaration of Independence. At the time it was a document which was received with wide-spread acclaim (but by a few with disdain). Since then, it has become a document that few refer to, for it has been largely forgotten.

If you have not read this document before, may I encourage you take note of its tolerance towards non-Jewish people. For Israel, this attitude of tolerance towards other people groups and nations – so long as

Israel's Declaration of Independence

they are prepared to respect and to live peaceably with Israel – originated at the time of Israel's Exodus from Egypt under the leadership of Moses.

"You shall neither mistreat a stranger nor oppress him, for you were strangers in the land of Egypt" (Exodus 22:21).

"And if a stranger dwells among you in your land, you shall not mistreat him. The stranger who dwells among you shall be to you as one born among you, and you shall love him as yourself; for you were strangers in the land of Egypt; I am the LORD your God" (Leviticus 19:33–34).

For non-Jewish people who have made their homes in Israel, they are made welcome and they experience freedom of religion and the opportunity of prosperity which many who live in neighboring countries do not enjoy or have access to.

If you have not been to Israel and you should decide to go; you will see that Israel welcomes those whose purpose is:

'To seek peace and pursue it' (Psalm 34:14).

****

The Complete Text of Israel's

DECLARATION OF INDEPENDENCE

ERETZ-ISRAEL was the birthplace of the Jewish people. Here their spiritual, religious and political identity was shaped. Here they first attained to statehood, created cultural values of national and universal significance and gave to the world the eternal Book of Books.

After being forcibly exiled from their land, the people kept faith with it throughout their Dispersion and never ceased to pray and hope for their return to it and for the restoration in it of their political freedom. Impelled by this historic and traditional attachment, Jews strove in every successive generation to re-establish themselves in their ancient homeland.

In recent decades they returned in their masses. Pioneers, ma'pilim (Hebrew – immigrants coming to Eretz-Israel in defiance of restrictive legislation) and defenders, they made deserts bloom, revived the Hebrew language, built villages and towns, and created a thriving community controlling its own economy and culture, loving peace but knowing how to defend itself, bringing the blessings of progress to all the country's inhabitants, and aspiring towards independent nationhood.

The Complete Text of Israel's Declaration of Independence

In the year 5657 (1897), at the summons of the spiritual father of the Jewish State, Theodore Herzl, the First Zionist Congress convened and proclaimed the right of the Jewish people to national rebirth in its own country. This right was recognized in the Balfour Declaration of the 2nd November, 1917, and re-affirmed in the Mandate of the League of Nations which, in particular, gave international sanction to the historic connection between the Jewish people and Eretz-Israel and to the right of the Jewish people to rebuild its National Home.

The catastrophe which recently befell the Jewish people – the massacre of millions of Jews in Europe – was another clear demonstration of the urgency of solving the problem of its homelessness by re-establishing in Eretz-Israel the Jewish State, which would open the gates of the homeland wide to every Jew and confer upon the Jewish people the status of a fully privileged member of the comity of nations.

Survivors of the Nazi holocaust in Europe, as well as Jews from other parts of the world, continued to migrate to Eretz-Israel, undaunted by difficulties, restrictions and dangers, and never ceased to assert their right to a life of dignity, freedom and honest toil in their national homeland.

In the Second World War, the Jewish community of this country contributed its full share to the struggle of the freedom – and peace-loving nations against the forces of Nazi wickedness and, by the blood of its soldiers and its war effort, gained the right to be reckoned among the peoples who founded the United Nations.

On the 29th November, 1947, the United Nations General Assembly passed a resolution calling for the establishment of a Jewish State in Eretz-Israel; the General Assembly required the inhabitants of Eretz-Israel to take such steps as were necessary on their part for the implementation of that resolution. This recognition by the United Nations of the right of the Jewish people to establish their State is irrevocable.

This right is the natural right of the Jewish people to be masters of their own fate, like all other nations, in their own sovereign State.

ACCORDINGLY WE, MEMBERS OF THE PEOPLE'S COUNCIL, REPRESENTATIVES OF THE JEWISH COMMUNITY OF ERETZ-ISRAEL AND OF THE ZIONIST MOVEMENT, ARE HERE ASSEMBLED ON THE DAY OF THE TERMINATION OF THE BRITISH MANDATE OVER ERETZ-ISRAEL AND, BY VIRTUE OF OUR NATURAL AND HISTORIC RIGHT AND ON THE STRENGTH OF THE RESOLUTION OF THE UNITED NATIONS GENERAL ASSEMBLY, HEREBY DECLARE THE ESTABLISHMENT OF A JEWISH STATE IN ERETZ-ISRAEL, TO BE KNOWN AS THE STATE OF ISRAEL.

The Complete Text of Israel's Declaration of Independence

WE DECLARE that, with effect from the moment of the termination of the Mandate being tonight, the eve of Sabbath, the 6th Iyar, 5708 (15th May, 1948), until the establishment of the elected, regular authorities of the State in accordance with the Constitution which shall be adopted by the Elected Constituent Assembly not later than the 1st October 1948, the People's Council shall act as a Provisional Council of State, and its executive organ, the People's Administration, shall be the Provisional Government of the Jewish State, to be called "Israel".

THE STATE OF ISRAEL will be open for Jewish immigration and for the Ingathering of the Exiles; it will foster the development of the country for the benefit of all its inhabitants; it will be based on freedom, justice and peace as envisaged by the prophets of Israel; it will ensure complete equality of social and political rights to all its inhabitants irrespective of religion, race or sex; it will guarantee freedom of religion, conscience, language, education and culture; it will safeguard the Holy Places of all religions; and it will be faithful to the principles of the Charter of the United Nations.

THE STATE OF ISRAEL is prepared to cooperate with the agencies and representatives of the United Nations in implementing the resolution of the General Assembly of the 29th November, 1947, and will take steps to bring about the economic union of the whole of Eretz-Israel.

WE APPEAL to the United Nations to assist the Jewish people in the building-up of its State and to receive the State of Israel into the comity of nations.

WE APPEAL – in the very midst of the onslaught launched against us now for months – to the Arab inhabitants of the State of Israel to preserve peace and participate in the upbuilding of the State on the basis of full and equal citizenship and due representation in all its provisional and permanent institutions.

WE EXTEND our hand to all neighboring states and their peoples in an offer of peace and good neighborliness, and appeal to them to establish bonds of cooperation and mutual help with the sovereign Jewish people settled in its own land. The State of Israel is prepared to do its share in a common effort for the advancement of the entire Middle East. WE APPEAL to the Jewish people throughout the Diaspora to rally round the Jews of Eretz-Israel in the tasks of immigration and upbuilding and to stand by them in the great struggle for the realization of the age-old dream – the redemption of Israel.

PLACING OUR TRUST IN THE ALMIGHTY, WE AFFIX OUR SIGNATURES TO THIS PROCLAMATION AT THIS SESSION OF THE PROVISIONAL COUNCIL OF STATE, ON THE SOIL OF THE HOMELAND, IN THE CITY OF TEL-AVIV, ON THIS SABBATH EVE, THE 5TH DAY OF IYAR, 5708 (14TH MAY,1948).

The Complete Text of Israel's Declaration of Independence

This (historic) document, setting out the reasons for and the aims and objectives of the returning exiles of Israel, was duly signed (and at the correct time) by Israel's first Prime Minister, David Ben-Gurion.

****

ABOUT THE AUTHOR

I was born in December 1943, but it was not until 1953 that my parents, my brother, my sister and I, started to attend Cranleigh Baptist Church (Surrey), and it was here we accepted Jesus as our Saviour.

My sister Clemaine had a very close relationship with Jesus, but as a result of a drowning accident Clemaine died on our family farm. At the time of her death, Clemaine had only recently started work in Guildford, Surrey, having just celebrated her fifteenth birthday. Although her death led to much family sorrow, our faith in God was never questioned.

Two years later I decided what I wanted to do when I left school. Six months later (June 1959) – I was just fifteen-and-a-half! – I joined the Royal Air Force to train as an aircraft electrician.

Initially as I moved from adolescence to adulthood, my faith in God was my anchor. Arrival in adulthood, however, can coincide with distractions, and it was weakness on my part that allowed other things to divert me away from my relationship with Jesus. Thankfully, the distractions failed to rob me of my faith, and the Holy Spirit needed only seven words (spoken by John the Baptist) to bring me back to Jesus. *"He must increase, but I must decrease."*

About the Author

Nearly fifteen years in the Royal Air Force was then followed by ten years with Rank Xerox as a photo-copier service engineer. Photo-copiers next gave way to *'Open Doors with Brother Andrew'*, a Christian organisation which was involved in taking Bibles to Christians in countries where expression of faith in God was restricted; such as China and the countries of Eastern Europe. At the end of my time with Open Doors (seven years), I joined Sun Life of Canada to train as a financial consultant (ten years). In the year 2000, I qualified as an Independent Financial Adviser.

With retirement looming, I decided to attempt a new venture, and so started *'Plus One Garden Services'* to help local people with their gardens and properties. I named this venture *'Plus One'* because of who Jesus is – He is my *'Plus One'*!

Many years ago, not long after I re-dedicated my life to Jesus, I remember attending an evening service at my home church in Cranleigh. The speaker took for his text, Hebrews 4:16 – *'Let us therefore come boldly to the throne of grace, that we may obtain mercy and find grace to help in time of need.'* It is a scripture I have never forgotten, and whenever I read it, it takes me back to Cranleigh.

Since that evening, and whenever I read Hebrews, I'm struck by its many references to the Old Testament, and because of this, my interest in both the Old Testament and Israel has been stimulated.

In one sense, I see Hebrews as the book on which the two historical periods of our Bibles are joined – BCE & CE. Also, the Jewish people span and connect these two periods. This may explain some of my fascination with Israel and the Jewish people.

From the time when Janet and I were married (1966), we have been interested in the history of the Jewish people and the Jewish nation. The Bible has been our primary means of understanding Israel, for it is here we have learnt about God's covenant with Abraham and his descendants – Abraham's stars.

Janet and I have visited Israel a number of times and have really enjoyed our visits. We have discovered Israel is a country you can easily fall in love with, and its people, mostly Jews and Arabs, are friendly and welcoming. In June 2007, we again visited Israel, and it was here I had an interesting experience.

As we were walking through the Arab quarter of the Old City of Jerusalem, I paused to take photographs. It was while I was viewing the architecture of some of the buildings of this city, where Jesus once walked, that I noticed an elderly Arab man. Unavoidably, like the beam of a laser, our eyes met, yet I had no awareness of his intention; if indeed he had one.

With a sense of purpose the man walked towards me. Next, as we faced each other, the stranger took hold of my right arm and looked into my eyes. His look was

About the Author

friendly, and so I was not afraid. Then his lips moved, and he spoke just four words: *"You are a Jew!"* I was dumbfounded, rooted to the spot! The man then removed his hand from my arm and walked away – never to be seen again. His timing was forty years to the day from when the Old City of Jerusalem was returned to the custodianship of the Jewish people.

Did his announcement change my life? I'm not sure, but I've not forgotten him! For many years I have believed that in my family's past, Jewish antecedents do exist, but I've not pursued the matter.

In believing pragmatism is in-tune with how I read and understand Scripture, I feel my usefulness to God is to try to understand the Hebrew Scriptures. This is why the foundations of what Christians believe is so important – together with the historical record of the Jewish people and the nation of Israel.

I pray, therefore, that what I have written – including the scriptures I have quoted and what others have said –will assist those who wish to understand the Jewish people and why God has restored them to the land named after their ancestor Jacob (Israel).

****

BIBLIOGRAPHY

Benjamin, M. *Last Days in Babylon.* London: Bloomsbury 2007.

Bullinger, E. W. *Number in Scripture.* Grand Rapids, MI: Kregel, 1967.

Churchill, W. S. *The Second World War Volume I. The Gathering Storm.* Cassell & Co. Ltd. 1948.

Elias, R. *Triumph of Hope – From Theresienstadt and Auschwitz to Israel.* Oxford: Wiley, 1998.

Grubb, N. P. *Rees Howells Intercessor.* Cambridge: Lutterworth, 1952.

Gryn, H. *Chasing Shadows.* London: Penguin, 2001.

Hardman, Rev. L. *The Survivors – The story of the Belsen Remnant.* London; Portland, OR: Vallentine Mitchell, 1958.

Herzl, T. *The Jewish State.* New York: Dover Publications, 1988.

Hodge, C. December 27, 1797 – June 19, 1878.

Hunting, J. *Israel – A Modern Miracle.* Murrumbeena: The David Press, 1969.

Josephus. *The Wars of the Jews.* Translated by G. A Williamson. London: Penguin, 2006.

Price, R. *Fast Facts on the Middle East Conflict.* 2003.

Price, C. *Focus on the Bible – Matthew.* Christian Focus, 1998.

Spurgeon, C. H. *'The Restoration and Conversion of the Jews'*. Sermon delivered on June 16, 1864 at the Metropolitan Tabernacle, Newington, London.

Taylor, F. *Dresden*. London: Bloomsbury, 2004.

United Nations Special Committee on Palestine. *'Report to the General Assembly of the United Nations. Lake Success, New York. 3rd September 1947'*.

****

HEBREW FOUNDATIONS OF THE CHRISTIAN FAITH

My other book which is being published by Apostolos Publishing looks at some the Old Testament's detail of the Hebrew Foundations of the Christian Faith.

When others show appreciation for what we do, it is encouraging; and so I include below an extract from the Foreword for this book. For full details, please contact Apostolos Publishing. Details can be found at the front of this book

An Extract from the Foreword

When I was invited to read the manuscript for this new book, I was impressed on a number of levels. David's book gives a thorough foundation upon which the new believer and student of the Bible can gain biblical orientation which points to Jesus Christ.

I have read similar studies of Old Testament themes which relate to New Testament theology, and so was particularly blessed that the focus was on Jesus Christ as the true revelation of the Old Testament. That there can be a temptation by authors to launch into a closed-circled theological explanation, without making and pointing to the real application – to the living out of the application in the power of the Holy Spirit – makes David's book highly relevant as a valuable resource.

The presence of the Holy Spirit and the kingdom of God are themes which can transform the course of our study, and David's book will, with certainty, be helpful in equipping believers in living fully in God's economy.

The employment in this book of induction questions – to draw in the student to dialogue and thinking about the topics and the ramifications thereof – is important if we are to see God reveal His Word to men and women, and not only pass on something of what we have learnt; though it may be perfectly valid.

I believe the use of this book would be a wonderful complement to any syllabus of teaching and education in a seminary or Bible school setting. David's book gives form without bondage, freedom without license, and sends the right message of a biblical witness to the living Lord Jesus.

Niall MacTaggart
Spruce Grove, Alberta, Canada

www.ingramcontent.com/pod-product-compliance
Lightning Source LLC
Chambersburg PA
CBHW071435160426
43195CB00013B/1909